Homeward

Homeward

Healing Our Separation from God and Each Other

Sandra Mayo

Foreword by Julia Wattacheril

CASCADE *Books* • Eugene, Oregon

HOMEWARD
Healing Our Separation from God and Each Other

Copyright © 2026 Sandra Mayo. All rights reserved. Except for brief quotations in critical publications or reviews, no part of this book may be reproduced in any manner without prior written permission from the publisher. Write: Permissions, Wipf and Stock Publishers, 199 W. 8th Ave., Suite 3, Eugene, OR 97401.

Cascade Books
An Imprint of Wipf and Stock Publishers
199 W. 8th Ave., Suite 3
Eugene, OR 97401

www.wipfandstock.com

PAPERBACK ISBN: 979-8-3852-5097-4
HARDCOVER ISBN: 979-8-3852-5098-1
EBOOK ISBN: 979-8-3852-5099-8

Cataloguing-in-Publication data:

Names: Mayo, Sandra, author. | Wattacheril, Julia, foreword.

Title: Homeward : healing our separation from God and each other / Sandra Mayo ; foreword by Julia Wattacheril.

Description: Eugene, OR : Cascade Books, 2026 | Includes bibliographical references.

Identifiers: ISBN 979-8-3852-5097-4 (paperback) | ISBN 979-8-3852-5098-1 (hardcover) | ISBN 979-8-3852-5099-8 (ebook)

Subjects: LCSH: Biographies. | Christian biography. | Christian biography United States. | Spiritual biography. | Spiritual biography United States.

Classification: BR1725.M39 A3 2026 (paperback) | BR1725.M39 (ebook)

VERSION NUMBER 01/30/26

Scripture quotations are from the ESV® Bible (The Holy Bible, English Standard Version®), © 2001 by Crossway, a publishing ministry of Good News Publishers. Used by permission. All rights reserved. The ESV text may not be quoted in any publication made available to the public by a Creative Commons license. The ESV may not be translated in whole or in part into any other language.

With honor and glory to the One who heals.

Contents

Foreword by Julia Wattacheril | ix
Preface | xiii

Introduction: Finding Home | 1

1. Keep the Second Half | 13
2. Embrace Disruptive Tensions | 25
3. Test the Strength of Your Rope | 37
4. Be a Salve | 49
5. Share History, Share His Story | 61
6. Know Your Opponent | 74
7. Remember and Forget, Constructively | 86

Conclusion: A Prayer for the Journey Home | 97

Appendix: A Practical Guide | 109
Acknowledgments | 127
Bibliography | 129

Foreword

WE ARE DIVIDED. TRUST is low. These are many of the sentiments I hear (and read) regarding the current state of our republic and increasingly, our world. Juxtaposed are enthusiastic comments about transformative technology and the potential for advancement of humanity, at least for some. The world of biomedical sciences and medicine, where I spend my professional life, provides a vantage point with equal parts urgency and frustration, grief, and hope—providing evidence to corroborate some of those sentiments and belie others. How do we show up at moments like these?

In *Homeward*, Sandy Mayo provides us with insights and experiences like a trustworthy sister. She leads us through story, sharing her own and revealing how knowing ourselves and our origins and remaining open to our own histories (all parts of them) can help us navigate the murky waters of division, denial, and even hatred manifest in our world today. She calls us to heal, together.

Learning often requires discomfort, especially in the second half of life. Dr. Mayo leads us through the navigable waters of our inner darkness, while holding the flashlight. *Homeward* helps us find ourselves and one another, so we can indeed behold a vision of what moving forward together in a broken and racially divided world by the power of the Holy Spirit might resemble. She bears the wisdom of one who knows themselves well enough to accept missteps and learn from them—and stays committed to the unending work because her vision is centered in the kingdom of God.

Foreword

For those readers craving a glimpse through the gospel lens on the work of reconciliation—of which there are few examples of lasting structural change given human idolatry and an ostensibly insatiable appetite for power—she begins to give light and edge to the initial steps, guided by scripture and self-reflection. Perhaps you will also take up boxing again like I did after being inspired by her to advance and engage in the ring, on a heavy bag, or in relationships that need healing.

Dr. Mayo and first I met each other wearing academic hats but bearing curious souls; she reached out after a podcast episode on "Suffering, Healing and Meaning" I had done during the SARS-CoV-2 pandemic as a physician in New York City (fun fact: my office sits in the very building where she was born). After a brief video call, I knew I had met someone I trusted. She had the listening skills of a therapist while sitting in the offices of institutional leadership at a time of increasing intensity for all things academic, socio-political, and economic.

Sandy is an accomplished educator, a university administrator, with titles in the offices of the provost and president—levels of institutional leadership that come with great responsibility. As she guides, you will encounter her subtly powerful stewardship of the space—the psychological space of unpacking how and what you think and the heartspace of trusting someone to help you see more clearly. Her attunement to your needs will be palpable, particularly with the gentle yet direct curiosity in the questions she poses at the end of each chapter. We all benefit from her skills as an educator and leader, but also from her friendship. We don't journey homeward solo.

On a recent trip, I was reminded of a story commonly attributed to anthropologist Margaret Mead and her dialogue with a student:

> Student: "What is the earliest sign of civilization?"
> The student expected her to say a clay pot, a grinding stone, or maybe a weapon.
> Margaret Mead thought for a moment, then she said, "A healed femur."

Foreword

A femur is the longest bone in the body, linking hip to knee. In societies without the benefits of modern medicine, it takes about six weeks of rest for a fractured femur to heal. A healed femur shows that someone cared for the injured person, did their hunting and gathering, stayed with them, and offered physical protection and human companionship until the injury could mend.

Mead explained that where the law of the jungle—the survival of the fittest—rules, no healed femurs are found. "The first sign of civilization is compassion, seen in a healed femur."

The timeliness of this book is part of its impact. In a world desperate for healers, particularly for ones who are in intimate contact with their woundedness as a point of connection to others, Sandy does the gently incisive work of getting us into a space to learn. You will be blessed to digest it, hopefully in dyads or groups, as so much good growth happens in community. Certainly our cultural wounds beg for salves with practical impact and applied with a tender touch—my prayer is that you'll receive it.

I bless you as you read this book. May you join a world of wounded healers who seek to head homeward together.

Julia Wattacheril, MD, MPH

Preface

My Dear Grandsons,

    I am writing this letter not knowing if you will ever read it, but it's best that I write it anyway.

    One day you might have questions about why I chose to write a book about race and faith, separation and healing. You might wonder about the experiences I share in the pages that follow. I imagine those experiences will be peculiar to you. After all, our lives are simply stitched together by hugs and kisses, laughter and smiles, and outdoor adventures and birthday surprises.

    I'm not sure what you understand about our racial differences—that I am Black, and you are White. I imagine you don't care much. And if asked, I am confident you would share some of the greatest unpolished wisdom the world has ever known about what it means to be connected by the bonds of family and the power of love.

    I know it would never occur to you that when you introduced me to your pet fish, Lewis and Clark, my mind secretly drifted into thoughts about buying you a third fish and naming it York. Not because Lewis and Clark aren't perfectly fine fish on their own. They certainly are, and I love that their names are straight out of your history lessons. But I think about York, too, knowing there's a chance you may not be familiar with his story. You see, I think about all the stories that are untold or lesser known. I think about them individually and collectively and the desert places of American history that remain desolate and dry.

Preface

I believe stories humanize the past and make us less indifferent to one another. I still want to believe that when we know someone's story, we are incapable of ignoring their inherent dignity and worth. In the chambers of my heart, I know otherwise—that we can receive the account of another and still deny their common personhood. Hopefully, not willfully so. I am writing this letter so that willful ignorance will never be your plight.

I pray that you experience the gift of an expansive and receptive curiosity for as long as possible. I love your ambitious questions. To inquire with hope and trust is a superpower. I am in awe that your wonderings have real question marks at the end. Your attentiveness will serve you well as you begin to make meaning of race and its deceptions. I'm not sure what that exploration will look like for you, but I can be certain it will be different from my own.

I entered the world long before you, in a time and place you will never know firsthand. My reflections on race and faith and the things that divide are from a specific vantage point. I am the child of immigrants. I was born in New York City in the first decade following the civil rights movement. I was part of the MTV generation that discovered its cultural aesthetic through televised music videos. I navigated childhood and adolescence without cell phones and social media. For the first half of my life, international news was transmitted through the evening television broadcast, and local news was delivered to the doorstep. As neighbors and citizens, we received much of the same information at the same time. Algorithms had not yet filtered our realities or amplified our differences.

Things seem more polarized today than ever before. But I imagine each generation might echo this sentiment. My mom and dad came to the United States during widespread protests against the Vietnam War and growing social and political tensions. Your Poppy and I will forever remember the September 11, 2001, terrorist attacks and ensuing clashes over issues of national security. Your parents came of age during the presidential elections of Barack Obama and Donald Trump, which laid bare our nation's

Preface

long-standing ideological and cultural fault lines in ways that were at once familiar and unrecognizable. Yours is the generation of the COVID-19 pandemic, which has both mirrored and magnified our ruptures.

It remains to be seen how our current divides will be described in future history books. I know how I might describe them. Yet had I known this present moment would be this present moment, I would have been hesitant to write this book. The gift of not knowing gave me permission to share freely from a place of desperate and abiding hope.

This book is a result of that hope, and I leave it to you.

Nana loves you.

Introduction
Finding Home

Because you have made the Lord your dwelling place—the
Most High, who is my refuge—no evil shall be allowed
to befall you, no plague come near your tent.

Psalm 91:9–10 ESV

Starting the Journey

From my half-cracked door, I could see my father across the hallway kneeling at his bedside, hands clasped and head bowed. Slowly waking, I watched through the haziness of my thoughts and vision. I knew my father was a praying man, but I had never seen him in this posture—childlike, humble, and meek, yet resolute. I found myself studying him. His stillness. His reverence. His dedication and obedience. I imagined the conversation he was having with God. I could almost hear his petitions.

This was the day we planned to drive through the Blue Mountains of Kingston, Jamaica, to the local regions nearest my paternal grandfather's birthplace. There was only a small chance he was alive still. We had no specific address or destination, just a hope-inspired path of our own. I never asked, so I don't know for sure, but it would not surprise me if my father had been praying for God to lead him home. His prayer may have been one of forgiveness for the father who abandoned him. Maybe he was asking for peace in his heart if he didn't find him. I wondered if his prayer was for the beginning of a new relationship or closure of the one he never had. Perhaps it was all or none of these things.

But isn't that what prayer is? A turning of our hearts and minds to the God of all peace and comfort. A surrender to the One who reigns in all our circumstances. A declaration of faith in God's power to do the impossible. Whatever my father prayed that morning, the look on his face said, "It is well with my soul." As he stood and turned to leave the room, I could sense the confidence in his step. My father always had a bounce and swagger to his walk—one that made him conspicuous in a crowd. On this particular morning, there was also a humble fortitude.

Searching for Home

We headed out early with our driver. Each time we reached a small community, my father would turn to the eldest person and ask the same question, "Do you know a man by the name John Richards? That's my father." Some of the individuals we approached quickly let us know the name was unfamiliar. Others lingered on the question as they considered the many names stored in their memories. Each time a person paused before responding, there was a moment of possibility. We eventually encountered a group of community members who had once known my grandfather. Yet, the ties were so minimal and long ago, we could find no meaningful path forward. After continuous dead ends and realizing that any traces of family in that area were now gone, we ended our search. I felt both disappointment and sadness and wondered how my father would respond. As I looked to his face, I saw the same peace from his morning prayer. I could exhale.

The following day, we visited the National Archives and University of West Indies Library. For some time, I had been researching the boys' home where my father grew up. This was an opportunity to gather some of the historical documents I located in my search. I was grateful to find a few remaining yearbooks. I

Introduction

knew my father sang in the choir, so I flipped through the pages to see if I could identify him among the many young boys. There he was. It had to be him. It looked like him. The image was hazy, and there were no names listed under the photo, but I was certain, or at least certain enough, to present it to my father. He was quick to identify himself. I could see his delight as he showed it to others. It was the only picture my father had of himself as a little boy.

That one photo helps narrate the story of my father's life and is part of a larger story about family, culture, race, nationhood, and the things that separate us. Both of my parents' stories are part of a larger historical narrative, one that emerges from the chasms left by slavery and colonialism, a history characterized by missing and scattered pieces. Both of my parents were born and lived in Jamaica through their early adulthood before arriving in the United States in 1968. Neither parent grew up with their parents. My father was a social orphan. Although he had one living parent, that parent was absent from his life. After being taken into custody by the state, my father was placed in the Alpha Boys' Home, a Catholic reform school founded in the decades following the emancipation of slavery and just one year after a government-commissioned inquiry into the condition of "juvenile vagrancy."[1] My mother, on the other hand, was a barrel child, a term used in the Caribbean—primarily during the late 1940s through the early 1960s—to describe children whose parents migrated to the mother country for work and sent material goods home to their children in barrel shipments.

Belonging to Him

From early childhood, I had questions about my family abroad and the Jamaica my parents called home. As a first-generation American, I lived with one foot inside the world I knew in the US and one foot out, seeking to reconcile pieces that rarely cohered. I was both the child of my parents who enjoyed the sounds of calypso and taste of fried plantains and callaloo and the product of

---

1. Jamaica Government Printing Office, *Report of the Commissioners*, 1.

my surroundings in New York and New Jersey where I consumed Italian hoagies and the music of Bruce Springsteen and Billy Joel. I was both the tranquil sensibility of my mother's Treasure Beach upbringing and the more boisterous expressions of my Northeastern life.

I loved going to the Caribbean markets in Brooklyn and purchasing fresh patties and hardo (hard dough) bread. It was a special treat when my father bought Jamaican sweets in the form of gizzada and grater cake. I particularly enjoyed when he sat in our backyard with his machete to cut pieces of sugarcane from the market for us to chew. When I was old enough to understand that most of my peers did not eat strange foods or have fathers who carried a machete, my delight turned to self-consciousness and curiosity. I developed a peculiar obsession with a search for the meaning of home, identity, and belonging.

Perhaps it was not so peculiar. Perhaps there is something about the human spirit that cries out for undividedness. This was God's intent for us before the fall. In the garden of Eden, we find the architectural design of God's plan for unity and wholeness. The garden was a place of God's presence. It was a place of endless provision and fruitfulness. It was a place of communion and fellowship. It was the place where Adam and Eve were made in the image of God, perfectly whole and without blemish. When they sinned, what was once fully intact and knitted with God's will became fractured. As the descendants of Adam and Eve, we are born into this state—separated from one another and from God, our one true home.

As disciples of Jesus our life becomes one of journeying back home. When we accept the gift of salvation, God initiates a process of restoration that continues to unfold through our faith and reliance on his power. When we humble ourselves in an act of worship or prayer, we proclaim our true home. As we come to know the Father more deeply, we gain capacity to love our brothers and sisters and strengthen the familial bonds through Jesus Christ with a love that unifies and perfects.

INTRODUCTION

Jesus's very nature is unity with the Father and Holy Spirit. He desires that we reflect the oneness of the Trinity and bear witness to God's love in the world:

> I do not ask for these only, but also for those who will believe in me through their word, that they may all be one, just as you, Father, are in me, and I in you, that they also may be in us, so that the world may believe that you have sent me. The glory that you have given me I have given to them, that they may be one even as we are one, I in them and you in me, that they may become perfectly one, so that the world may know that you sent me and loved them even as you loved me. (John 17:20–23 ESV)

Why would Jesus pray these words in the garden of Gethsemane? Why was it so important to Jesus that he seal the bond of unity before his death? The timing is not inconsequential. We know from Jesus's prayer that the bond of unity is something divinely knit in the hearts of believers. It is not of our doing. It is not of our own goodness or capacity. It is by his glory, given of God, granted as a gift of grace. It is a gift we must receive by faith and keep by faith.

This prayer is a moment we see Jesus's heart on display. These are some of Jesus's final words as the time draws near for him to fulfill his mission on earth, so we must understand that these words, and our response to them, are central to that mission. It is important to understand that Jesus completed his work of restoration on the cross. With or without us, it is finished—the undoing of separation has already been made possible. Through his sacrifice, we have access to the Father. We can enter covenantal relationship with God and each other. We have the capacity to live as one as Jesus and the Father are one in shared purpose and mission, putting God's glory—his full splendor and majesty—on display through our unity. Our oneness becomes our witness.

When I speak about unity, I am not referring to sameness. That which is already the same and singular does not need to be unified. By definition, unity is the joining of separate parts into one. In military terms, unity of command refers to the joining of separate forces under one authority.² As faithful sojourners, we are baptized into one body, under the authority of Jesus Christ, our one commander in chief (1 Cor 12:13).

Unity and wholeness are not synonymous, but they are related. While unity refers to the joining together in a single mission, under one authority, wholeness refers to the completeness and flourishing made possible as we pursue communal relationship with God.

Receiving Wholeness

When my brother was a little boy, he had an extreme aversion to slices of bread with holes. If my mother placed a slice of toast with holes on his plate at breakfast, he would refuse to eat it. With three children, with very different temperaments, my poor mother endured more than her fair share of idiosyncrasies. Really, a hole in the bread? It was the kind of moment that rattles a parent. In the busyness of morning and making every effort to feed, dress, and get everyone off to school, the last thing my mom had time or patience for was trying to convince a four-year-old there was nothing wrong with the bread. In his eyes, it was broken, flawed, and insufficient to fill his hunger.

His tears and frustration were so effusive, it was as though he took personal offense at the inadequacy of the bread. There was no convincing him it was okay. The longer the broken bread sat in front of him, the more his displeasure grew. My mother eventually devised a strategy that would satisfy the most irrational toddler tantrum. In a stroke of brilliance, she plugged his toast by tearing a small piece from her own, patching my brother's piece, and filling the space that was missing.

Perhaps my mom should never have given in to toddler demands, but I think we have all, at one time or another, traded our parental authority for peace, even for a moment. Setting that aside

---

2. Strain, "Unity of Command."

INTRODUCTION

and looking through the eyes of my little brother, I know that all he could see was a flawed and broken piece of bread set before him.

There is something about us that seeks wholeness. We want it in our families, in our communities, in nature, in ourselves. God wants it too. God's design is wholeness with him and with others. This desire for wholeness is woven into our very calling:

> All this is from God, who reconciled us to himself through Christ and gave us the ministry of reconciliation: that God was reconciling the world to himself in Christ, not counting people's sins against them. And he has committed to us the message of reconciliation. (2 Cor 5:18–19 ESV)

Scripture tells us that we are part of the same family (Acts 17:26) and by salvation we are brought into one fellowship (Gal 3:28). Even though we are made in the image of God, brought together as one family, that doesn't mean conflict won't arise. It will. Throughout the Scriptures, we see conflict among the disciples (Acts 15:36–41), between brothers (Gen 25:21–26), between father and son (2 Sam 15), and within the church (see Paul's letters to the church in Corinth).

A few years ago, I found myself amid conflict as members of the Christian university where I worked debated the rightness or wrongness of our statement on human sexuality. As the chief diversity officer at Seattle Pacific University, I was often asked to speak into matters of institutional policy related to hiring, retention, and workplace belonging. At the height of the debate, these policy conversations became emotionally and spiritually weighty, and agreement seemed to pull beyond our reach.

At my then home in Seattle, I had a picture window with beautiful views of the Puget Sound. I spent a lot of hours by that window. It's where I would go to God in protest and in prayer. One afternoon, I looked across the white-capped water marveling at God's creation. My eyes welled with tears as I sensed his presence despite the warring in my heart. In my frustration and desperation for a way out or way forward, I found myself uttering inaudibly, "This is not my battle!" I could hardly finish the thought before God whispered to me, "But I have you here." I sobbed in my exhaustion. I sobbed in relief. Even though it wasn't the response I wanted, I could rest knowing he was with me.

"But I have you here." Those five words were the beginning of a new understanding of the God who calls us to unity and wholeness. God often has us in situations not to reveal an answer, but to reveal himself. Stories don't always have happy endings. Agreement is not always found. Peace is not always made. Relationships are not always healed. Yet, we can faithfully live the call to unity and wholeness knowing that with each act of surrender we will come to know Emmanuel, God with us. It is in this knowing we learn to imitate his perfected love. God is perfectly whole and holy. As we are created in his image, we are to be whole. This wholeness includes a healed vision of who we are in Christ, individually and collectively.

Living in God, Our Home

It is this process of returning home to a state of unbroken wholeness that is the subject of this book. I am writing for those who long to return home, who share a peculiar obsession with wholeness. I want to reach those who are tired and weary of sensationalized headlines that lead us to greater distrust, fear, and dividedness and those who need a refreshing of their soul toward a kingdom vision of reconciliation and repair. I also desire an audience among those who are skeptical about the possibility of a peaceable world across dividing lines and among those who have questions but are afraid to ask. Ultimately, this book is intended for all who are curious about what it might look like to live together in a world of difference with a truth-telling and healing love that can sustain us in covenant community. I pray that this book will provide a way forward for every person who wants to live boldly into a life of forgiveness and grace, and be drawn into a wholeness that is the kingdom of God.

There is a way home, a way to unity, and it is found at the cross. My desire in writing this book is that it would point us to

Introduction

Jesus Christ and encourage full surrender. That it would help us emulate Christ and pursue his heart in all relationships. That together we would experience the beauty and freedom of Christ's love revealed in John 17.

Dwelling Together

The following chapters share lessons learned from my own journey through race and faith. In what is part autobiography and part cultural analysis, I invite readers into ordinary stories across childhood, marriage, parenting, and vocation to reveal the heart of an extraordinary God. The book is just that—an invitation to relationship, understanding, and hope with a desire to focus on the One who can orient our hearts toward the love that restores all things. The main chapters introduce a set of redemptive moves—small but purposeful acts—that can inch us closer to God and each other that we might be transformed in his image.[3]

Chapter 1, "Keep the Second Half," highlights and amplifies the latter part of God's twofold commandment to love the Lord and love our neighbors. Love of neighbor cannot be theoretical; it must be personal and firsthand. It must also extend panoramically with an understanding that the object of God's love is his whole creation—every land, every people. The mandate is clear. We are all neighbors. There is no cultural stranger.

Chapter 2, "Embrace Disruptive Tensions," encourages us to not flee from the conflict and misunderstandings that will arise when we engage across racial and cultural differences. Jesus wants to disrupt the way we order our lives and relationships so we are no longer at enmity with him or one another. Working toward this unity is a process of sanctification because we must die to ourselves for the sake of the gospel. It is a costly but worthy investment.

Chapter 3, "Test the Strength of Your Rope," examines the finite nature of our capacity to love. Despite our well-intended sentiments, our understanding of one another is often based on

---

3. The phrase "redemptive move" has been used by previous authors, including Andy Crouch in *The Life We're Looking For.*

a collection of ill-formed, untested assumptions that limit our capacity to see the image of God in each person with a limitless love. To experience the gift of unity and wholeness, we must allow our encounters across differences to be revelatory and transformative.

Chapter 4, "Be a Salve," argues that building racial empathy is a powerful and necessary step toward healing our separation from one another. Racial distance and suffering remain in the space between historic racism and its present-day residue. Racial distance and suffering grow in the absence of actively cooperating in God's plan to restore human dignity where it has been violated. We are to engage in this suffering toward a restored architecture of the human heart.

Chapter 5, "Share History, Share His Story," reminds us that we have an important role to play in telling the story of humankind with honesty and integrity. Distortions of history not only create an incomplete and inaccurate picture of our neighbors, but because our stories are interwoven with the grander narrative of God's story, historical myths also undermine our understanding of Christ's work in the world throughout time.

Chapter 6, "Know Your Opponent," teaches us how to fight rightly. If we understand our partnership with God in his work of bringing redemption and wholeness to all things, then our understanding of what it looks like to defeat our enemies requires a change of strategy—a spiritual shift that draws us into the power of God's victory over Satan and a relinquishing in our hearts of the desire to triumph over our earthly opponents.

Chapter 7, "Remember and Forget, Constructively," explores the duality of memory in walking toward unity. As reconcilers pursuing peace with God and each other, we have a responsibility to remember. We also have a responsibility to forget. This is not a contradiction. It is an opportunity to grasp God's grace and mercy while surrendering to the resurrection power of Christ.

INTRODUCTION

Accepting the Invitation

On earth, flesh will continue to war against spirit. It is the constant and ongoing battle, the root of all divisions on earth. There's no getting around it. Jesus predicts division. It is an inevitable part of our experience as sojourners living as temporary guests in our earthly dwelling. Yet, Christ also calls for unity among believers and makes a way through the cross—the place where divisions die, and God's love redeems. How can we reconcile these seemingly contradictory promises of division and unity, especially when the things that divide strike at the very core of our being? Racial hatred. Cultural fragmentation. Political friction. Moral disagreement. Church splitting.

In the chapters that follow, we will journey to the heart of a God who gave everything to restore relational wholeness.

HOMEWARD

> Because you have made the Lord your dwelling place—the Most High, who is my refuge—no evil shall be allowed to befall you, no plague come near your tent.
>
> PSALM 91:9–10 ESV

Reflection Questions

1. Read Ps 91:9. What does it mean that the Lord is our dwelling place, our home?
2. Have you ever been "homesick" for the Lord? What is the antidote to our homesickness?
3. What does John 17:20–23 reveal about God's desire for us to experience relational wholeness?

1

Keep the Second Half

> Jesus answered, "The most important is, 'Hear, O Israel: The Lord our God, the Lord is one. And you shall love the Lord your God with all your heart and with all your soul and with all your mind and with all your strength.' The second is this: 'You shall love your neighbor as yourself.' There is no other commandment greater than these."
>
> MARK 12:29–31 ESV

The Community Pool

NEW KIDS POPPED UP from every corner in our neighborhood. With all the pickup games of kickball that summer, I thought we had run into every kid within a one-mile radius. It was rare to see a new face, but on this July morning, strangers who would soon be friends filled our backyard. "Can we swim in your pool?" they asked my mom. These were the days before cell phones, so I'm not sure how word spread so quickly. It appears social networking is endemic to the human spirit.

I don't want to exaggerate how many kids were at our house that day. Memory has a strange way of multiplying exponentially those things that lie on the extremes of both good and bad. This happened to be one of those good memories, and so I imagine my mind tips in favor of amplifying the number. With precision I can state that before we knew it, a steady flow of young boys and girls made it to our home—one by one, and in twos and threes. There was no process for determining who would gain access. No one was turned away. We didn't have time or concern to do so. As kids, we lacked the sophistication to erect boundaries and barriers. Those things were beyond our simple desire to have fun.

And fun we had. We jumped and dove and immersed ourselves, allowing the cool water to sweep against our skin. The water was soft like air. The freedom of letting our bodies drift into its embrace felt like heaven. We took turns diving in, not in a headlong sort of way, but in an awkward leap-and-slide kind of motion. We couldn't all fit at the same time, but instinctively we took turns jumping in and out and assuming our position in the growing line. Upon each exit, we thought about how to make the next dive better than the previous. We watched each other and picked up a few tips along the way. If someone flopped, we adjusted. If someone entered gracefully, we mimicked their technique. It never got too technical, and the stakes never rose too high. It was a day for simple pleasures. You could count our joy in the currency of laughter and giggles. That morning provided all the right conditions for summer friendships that could last a lifetime.

My dad is long gone now, but while he was still with us, I wish I would have asked what prompted him to build a pool that summer morning. Had my siblings and I entreated him? I certainly don't remember spurring the idea. More likely, it was a product of my father's resourcefulness. Dad was a craftsman. He could build and do almost anything with his hands. He did particularly well with objects discarded as scraps. Dad was also an electrician by trade, so it wasn't unusual for him to store excess materials from completed jobs. As a young girl, I enjoyed scanning the shelves of our shed, which were lined with electrical boxes, conduit fittings, red-wing wire nuts, elbows, soldering wire, junction boxes, and all sorts of tools. Even though some of the materials in Dad's shop had already been used for their intended purpose, they never looked like junk to me. Even the metal punchouts looked like shiny half dollars. My brother and I would set them aside as coins and count our fortune with the adroitness of two well-established bankers. Life in our imagination was always full and rich.

I can only assume the idea for a homemade pool was a combination of Dad wanting to fulfill our need for carefree playfulness and living out his own desire for childhood fun. Somewhere in that intersection, the idea of a swimming pool was born. While the details have been lost in years gone by, I remember the gratification of watching my dad work. There were no hand-drawn plans or written instructions. Dad worked from something more innate, so I struggled to follow his pattern. As an observer, I simply watched with a restless excitement anticipating the next logical step in the building process.

For this particular creation, Dad used PVC pipe and connectors to erect the foundation. Next came the pool walls. He pulled out what appeared to be a heavy-duty clear plastic liner almost as thick as a tarp, but not quite. I neither knew nor cared what it was. If it could hold water, that was good enough for me. I don't know the size of the structure, but it was certainly big enough to capture my interest and convince me he was building a pool of respectable magnitude. As the pool took shape, my enthusiasm grew. I imagined the joy of jumping in the water for the first time. Surely, there would be lots of splashing. I could picture the water droplets reflecting the sun's rays. Undoubtedly, the sun would be outshone only by the brightness of our smiles. The rush of water against our bodies would be exhilarating, and although I didn't know how to swim, I imagined my amateur strokes would bring the reward of the water's cool embrace just the same. As our garden hose slowly filled the vessel, my heart swelled—the pool could not fill quickly enough. In the end, the reality was not far from what I imagined. As kids, the joy we experienced that summer day was unrivaled.

But not everyone was sharing in the delight. I learned much later that my mom was both nervous and mortified. Nervous that someone might get injured in our new pool. Mortified that we were calling it a pool and that the water was growing browner as each bare-footed child jumped into the freshly filled basin. It was a short-lived experiment. By the end of the day, my mom's pleading won out, and the pool was deconstructed.

Neighborliness and Fellowship

As I reflect on that day, what stands out most is the way that the pool drew a community of kids together. In its simplest form, this is what neighborliness looks like. Extending an open invitation. Demonstrating welcome. Making room where there is seemingly no room. Looking in the face of a stranger and knowing that we are inextricably linked. Encountering the stranger and discovering our proximity. Experiencing a shared humanity in the everyday joys and realizing our participation together is the essence of life.

Our innocence served as a bridge and indispensable guide to move us toward one another. Somehow, we knew that neighborliness included those we hadn't known previously. I'm not sure that we even learned each other's names by the end of the day. Neighborliness went beyond the need for formalities. The real connection was found in an unspoken understanding that life's smallest big moments are to be shared as we step freely into our common fellowship. In a rather trivial way, that day in our backyard exemplified the threads of neighborliness at the heart of the Great Commission.

Neighborliness, breaking down walls, is key to achieving unbroken wholeness in the kingdom of God. Without it, we cannot understand how to live relationally as a community of witnesses to the living gospel. If we are commissioned to bring individuals into direct relationship with Christ, we must reflect the nature and character of the One we serve, the One who proclaimed, "They will know us by our love." Neighborliness is the way we see and relate to one another when we understand that we exist because of

Keep the Second Half

God, for God, and to glorify God. It is the way by which we pierce the darkness and hostility of erected barriers.

This idea of neighborliness has captured my imagination for some time as I've navigated the dividing lines of race. The idea of what it means to be a neighbor became particularly compelling to me in the aftermath of the 2012 killing of Trayvon Martin, a Black teenager surveilled and ultimately shot to death by George Zimmerman, a neighborhood watchman who became suspicious of Trayvon, who was walking to his father's house. While many facts about the interaction between Trayvon Martin and George Zimmerman and the ensuing altercation, deadly shooting, and court proceedings have been contested, what particularly unsettles me is the initial suspicion that precipitated the cascade of events. It is common for residents to have visitors, so it is difficult to follow the logical path of a resident seeing an unfamiliar face to calling 911 and following the unknown individual especially when there is no imminent danger. Such action leaves unanswered questions:

- Should suspicion based on unfamiliarity become a justifiable cause for an escalated response?
- If so, have we created an intractable dilemma of the stranger as threat?
- Whom within our society does this put most at risk?
- Whom do we fail to see as our neighbor?

In Luke 10:29–37, Jesus makes it clear, our neighbor is everyone. Nothing can forfeit that gospel truth. So, what disqualified Trayvon from being a welcomed neighbor who evokes neither suspicion nor speculation?

On July 14, 2013, when America and the world learned of the verdict in the Trayvon Martin case, reactions varied widely—a feeling of relief from the Zimmerman family, a resolute expression of faith from the Martin family, and justifiable anger among Sanford community members.[1] Many agreed that even though

---

1. This discussion of the Trayvon Martin case is reproduced from my earlier work, Richards Mayo, "Chasing the 'Hounds of Hell,'" with permission.

Zimmerman's actions may have been legal under the Stand Your Ground law, the verdict did not appear to be just.

As I returned to Howard Thurman's *Jesus and the Disinherited* just weeks before the Zimmerman verdict, the author's exploration of the biblical principle of neighborliness struck me. Thurman was a Baptist minister and theologian who grew up in the South during the height of segregation and played a key role in shaping Martin Luther King Jr.'s nonviolent approach to civil rights. He was deeply concerned about the perniciousness of racial segregation in the South, and in *Jesus and the Disinherited*, he offered a prophetic gaze into the condition of the American heart and urged readers toward fellowship. Yet the kind of fellowship Thurman referred to can neither be a distant understanding established through third-person accounts, nor be established on superficial interactions that do not challenge existing patterns of racial separation. Rather, it must "be rooted in concrete experience."[2] As Thurman pointed out, "No amount of good feeling for people in general, no amount of simple desiring, is an adequate substitute."[3] Thurman described racial segregation as a "complete ethical and moral evil" because it obliterates any possibility of genuine fellowship through which individuals can come to understand their common humanity:[4]

> Whatever it may do for those who dwell on either side of the wall, one thing is certain: it poisons all normal contacts of those persons involved. The first step toward love is a common sharing of a sense of mutual worth and value. This cannot be discovered in a vacuum or in a series of artificial or hypothetical relationships. It has to be in a real situation, natural, free.[5]

Segregation, he argued, provides a moral justification that ultimately leads to hatred. Once unleashed, hatred cannot be contained and risks moving from a singular subject to a more general contempt. According to Thurman, hatred often develops when

2. Thurman, *Jesus and the Disinherited*, 106.
3. Thurman, *Jesus and the Disinherited*, 106.
4. Thurman, *Jesus and the Disinherited*, 98.
5. Thurman, *Jesus and the Disinherited*, 75.

there is "contact without fellowship."⁶ When lives are distanced by metaphorical and figurative walls, the outcome is almost certain: interactions marked by unfamiliarity, desensitized from a collective existence, and informed by stereotypes that deface the image of God in people.

The picture of racial segregation in America today is perhaps most vividly captured by Dustin Cable, a demographic researcher at the University of Virginia, who produced a comprehensive map of racial distribution in America. The racial dot map features 308,745,538 colored dots—one for each person counted in the 2010 census, with each racial group represented by a different color. This data visualization tool tells the story of each city—some show clear lines of demarcation between races; others show more of an overlapping between groups; and still others show almost complete racial homogeneity and isolation.⁷ Yet across all the maps, one thing is clear: although we are not as segregated as we were in the Jim Crow era, we are far from unified.

The retreat into safety that, in some measure, gives birth to gated communities like the one where Trayvon Martin was shot, may serve to compound segregation and its perils.⁸ Although it may never be possible to determine the true racial motivations in the Martin shooting, prevailing patterns of racial isolation in the United States, mingled with physical boundaries that demarcate difference and reinforce an insider-outsider divide, may be part of the deadly combination we continually witness.

The antidote, Thurman argues, must be fellowship: "Every man is potentially every other man's neighbor. Neighborliness is non-spatial; it is qualitative. A man must love his neighbor directly, clearly, permitting no barriers between."⁹

This all sounds good, but practically, how do we love the neighbor that we see as an enemy? The one who votes for the party we don't support. The one whose values oppose our own. The one

6. Thurman, *Jesus and the Disinherited*, 75.
7. Vanhemert, "Best Map Ever Made."
8. Benjamin, "Gated Community."
9. Thurman, *Jesus and the Disinherited*, 89.

whose front-lawn banner represents ideals we abhor. The one who wears a hoodie. How do we love the one we do not know? One of the greatest detriments of residential segregation is the physical, spiritual, and economic separation it created. Its historical residue still shapes, limits, and distorts our interactions. But if God requires us to be in fellowship with our neighbors, that also means he's made a way.

A Warm Welcome

I remember the stunned faces of friends when I said that I was moving from Seattle to East Texas. Texas?

Wow! The questions of concern, doubt, and condemnation flowed:

"Are you okay with that?"

"Where in Texas, exactly?"

"Gilmer, it's east of Dallas and Tyler?"

"Tyler. Isn't that where a Black man was lynched?" one friend asked.

"Will you be safe?" followed another.

I must admit, fear settled into my heart during those weeks leading up to my move. In the quiet of night, I would imagine worst-case scenarios: driving past Confederate flags on my way to work or encountering racial epithets.

After a thirty-three-hour drive from Seattle, I walked into my new home to find welcome gifts from our realtor—an assortment of local coffees, personalized mugs, a "Home Sweet Home" wall hanging, and a card that read:

> Jon and Sandra—I hope you truly love your decision to move to Texas. It has been my pleasure to serve you and work through this phase of your new journey. I hope you build lots of good memories in your new home.

I took those words in, and as I looked around at my new home, I cried joyfully.

Moments later, our neighbors stopped by to introduce themselves and welcome us to the neighborhood. They offered their assistance and gave us the name and phone numbers of two young men in the community who could help unload our PODS. Sure enough, as soon as church let out the next day, we had two twenty-somethings standing at our door ready to work. They shook our hands and without wasting any time asked, "Where would you like us to start?" to which I replied, "How much time do you have to offer your assistance?" Their only response, "As much time as it takes to get the job done, ma'am." As the four of us unloaded items from the PODS, I couldn't help but chuckle as I thought back to my fears, which now seemed irrational.

Shortly after Jon and I settled into our new home, we visited a local winery to celebrate my fiftieth birthday. We were seated outside on the patio listening to live music. A few minutes later, an unexpected rainstorm created a double rainbow. The band had to set up under the patio, and as luck would have it, right next to our table. We simultaneously had front row seats to nature's and the band's performances.

As guests pulled out their phones to capture the moment, cheer and goodwill filled the room. Tables greeted each other and remarked at the beauty we were witnessing. As we waited for food and drinks to arrive, some guests danced. Others sat at their tables humming, tapping, swaying, and singing to the music. I learned that the woman at the table behind us lost her husband eleven years ago. They always loved to dance, and she wished he could be there that night. I found out that the woman at the table to our right was celebrating her birthday. I discovered that one of the band members lives with and takes care of his ailing ninety-year-old mother. He acquired a love for music at the age of eight while visiting his aunt's house. She had a piano, and he sat at the keys and immediately composed a song. His aunt delivered the piano to his house the following day, and he's been playing ever since. That night, moments were created, stories shared, memories cherished and made.

The next day, one of our neighbors invited us to dinner. When we arrived, I was greeted by all our neighbor friends, a bouquet of flowers, and a birthday cake. People I hadn't known two months prior had gathered to celebrate a milestone in my life. These experiences are becoming commonplace for me and Jon, but I never want to describe them as ordinary. They're not, but they are made possible when we first understand our condition of estrangement.

Confederate Flags and a Restoring Grace

When sin was introduced, humankind was left without access to God. Separated from his presence and his grace, alienation and disunity were our fate. The moment Jesus died on the cross, "the curtain of the temple was torn in two from top to bottom. And the earth shook, and the rocks were split. The tombs also were opened" (Matt 27:51–52). Through the Gospel of John, we simply understand, "It is finished" (John 19:30). Three simple words signifying the carrying out of God's redemptive plan. The debt of sin forever paid. No more veil. No more separation. The ultimate victory won. Christ's sacrifice on the cross gave us access to fellowship with God but also required a life of fellowship with the body of Christ (1 Cor 12:27). The grace of God necessitates a shift in our hearts toward reconciliation, even when we disagree on the most fundamental issues.

Remember my fears of seeing Confederate flags on the way to work? My fears were not unfounded. While I don't see them on my route to work, they are displayed in front of several nearby homes. Despite the kindness of individuals in my community, there remains long-standing racial ignorance and a festering menace of White supremacy. Those things exist simultaneously. It is this paradoxical condition of the human experience that demands the kind of supernatural love God calls us to and empowers through the work of the Holy Spirit. As disciples of Christ, we can become conduits of his love, drawn into fellowship beyond all barriers. Pastor Paul Tripp puts it this way: "I move toward you not because I trust you. I move toward you knowing we're both broken, and

Keep the Second Half

this is potentially messy. I move toward you because there is hope for us because of the cross."[10]

Estrangement is no longer our affliction. We are freed from the life sentence of alienation. Through the indwelling of the Holy Spirit, we have capacity for agape love, a transcendent love that compels us toward one another. When I say *love*, I don't mean being endeared to everyone. That's simply not possible or even requisite to fulfilling our calling to love our neighbors as ourselves. The kind of love I'm talking about emanates from a deep wellspring of God's forgiveness and a desire to commune with him. We love not because we are good. We love not because we find ourselves in agreement with our neighbors. We love across the dividing lines because *God is so good*, and we must refuse to step back into the estrangement that separated us from his goodness. The same grace that restores us to Christ is the same grace that restores us to one another. God's grace is all-sufficient and all-abundant. The wholeness of grace awaits us, and we must steward God's grace wholly and fully in a way that our lives, individually and collectively, glorify him.

When we stand before the throne of God, we won't have a voter registration card indicating our party affiliation. We won't be asked to check a box specifying our race and ethnicity. There will be no record of how many likes we accumulated on our social media feeds. There will be no regard for the zip code we were born into, nor will we be rewarded for sequestering ourselves in fortress communities that provide a false sense of unity and faithfulness. We will, however, be accountable to how we lived out the greatest commandment—loving the Lord our God with all our heart, soul, mind, and strength, and loving our neighbor as ourselves. If we have any hope of experiencing the beauty of kingdom diversity and fullness of grace, we must surrender everything that might lead to our estrangement from God and from one another. We must embrace the wholeness of God in fellowship, navigating the world as children swimming in the same pool, receiving the gift of living water.

10. Tripp, "Your Walk With God."

Jesus answered, "The most important is, 'Hear, O Israel: The Lord our God, the Lord is one. And you shall love the Lord your God with all your heart and with all your soul and with all your mind and with all your strength.' The second is this: 'You shall love your neighbor as yourself.' There is no other commandment greater than these."

MARK 12:29–31 ESV

Reflection Questions

1. Read Mark 12:30–31. Is it possible to love God without loving our neighbor? Is it possible to love our neighbor without loving God?

2. Do you agree with Howard Thurman's analysis that genuine fellowship must be rooted in concrete experience? If so, what does this mean for you as you actively choose to live out the greatest commandment?

3. Thurman explained that hatred often begins when there is *contact without fellowship*. What do you think he means by this statement? Can you think of specific examples from history and in our current moment where this principle is illustrated?

2

Embrace Disruptive Tensions

> In the temple he found those who were selling oxen and sheep and pigeons, and the money-changers sitting there. And making a whip of cords, he drove them all out of the temple, with the sheep and oxen. And he poured out the coins of the money-changers and overturned their tables. And he told those who sold the pigeons, "Take these things away; do not make my Father's house a house of trade." His disciples remembered that it was written, "Zeal for your house will consume me."
>
> JOHN 2:14–17 ESV

A Radical Experiment

WHEN I MET MY husband Jon more than twenty years ago, we embarked on a pretty radical experiment to bring together two very different lives. I'm not talking about the fact that he is White, and I am Black, or that he is six-foot-three and I am five-foot-five. Those differences were negligible in comparison as we learned each other's life stories. The more palpable differences resulted from what

I'll call our *cultural milieu*. Jon came from an upper-middle-class family; his father was bi-vocational—a pastor and pacemaker specialist. Jon was born and raised in Southern California. He grew up in church, attended private schools, and was captain of his football team and chaplain of his high school. In college, he lived in Newport Beach, California, where he would surf in the morning before class and ski in the winter on vacations at his family cabin in Mammoth, California. On any given day, if you ask my husband how he is doing, his typical response will be "Faaan-taaastic." Jon cannot be characterized as "glass half empty" or "glass half full." He is "glass overflowing," and the world is all aglow.

To be fair, I'm not "glass half empty" or "glass half full" either. I'm more, "What glass?" Cynically approaching the world, I prefer to ask, "If a glass truly exists, who gets to drink from it? Equity, please." I grew up in New Jersey, and as the daughter of Jamaican immigrants, we had all the necessities of life, but extras were . . . well, extras, and there were few. I was definitely shaped more by my parents' Caribbean sensibilities than by the Jersey Shore culture that surrounded me. My childhood was fun, unhurried, rustic, and filled with imaginative possibilities. One of the things I remember most about childhood was building things out of ordinary items. Little did I know, and it was only later in life I discovered, that building a trap out of chicken wire, twine, and a stick to catch a pet rabbit was something my New Jersey peers did not share with me. (Don't worry, we released the rabbit that same day, but the idea of building everything with our hands was true to our Jamaican roots).

Thus, the beginning of the differences between me and my husband. But differences aside, our experiment was well on its way. To add to the complexity, when I married Jon, I became the stepmom to an eight-year-old girl, Victoria, and an eleven-year-old boy, Jonathan, and they both had very different responses to me.

Victoria embraced me right away. In fact, when I accepted her father's proposal, she immediately exclaimed, "Yay! Another girl in the house." She welcomed me with open arms and started planning all the girly things we would do together—getting our nails done,

Embrace Disruptive Tensions

going shopping, baking, doing arts and crafts. Victoria's embrace was full, complete, innocent, genuine, generous, and unconditional. She connected with ease, loved with excitement, observed intently, and sought opportunities to steal away my attention.

Jonathan took a different approach. He had some very specific relational conditions (some tensions, let's say)—three to be exact. First and most importantly, I would have to watch the *Lord of the Rings* trilogy with him . . . all twelve hours. I enjoy movies, like most everyone else, but my taste is more real-life-inspired dramas and historic biographies. Fantasy adventure films, not so much. But I was all in and I figured, "How bad could it be?" Quietly I thought to myself, "He's an eleven-year-old boy, surely he'll lose interest along the way." What I didn't know is that Jonathan had already watched the trilogy several times, had somewhat of a photographic memory, could recall scenes and memorize lines with incredible precision, and had an extraordinary ability to interpret themes and symbols. So, throughout the movie, at each significant moment of rising action, he paused the movie, turned to me, and posed a series of questions to gauge my understanding of the growing plot, and in essence, test my commitment to this new relationship.

Second condition—Jonathan had very specific instructions as to how I was to care for his dog, Cookie. One week when Jon was traveling to the East Coast on a business trip, he asked if I could stay at the house with the kids. Again, I thought . . . no problem. I'll get them off to school, pick them up in the afternoon, make dinner, and handle homework. "I can do this!" And besides, it was good practice for the soon-to-be realities of our new life together. So, as I was making breakfast and preparing to take the kids to school that first morning, what was foremost on Jonathan's mind was that I appropriately care for his dog while he was at school. His instructions went something like this: "Now, Cookie must be fed twice a day, and what she really likes is to have her soft food mixed with her hard food. And when you do this, take what's left on the spoon, hold it in front of her, and let her lick the spoon. She *really* likes to lick the spoon." I learned later from his father that spoon-feeding the puppy was definitely not part of the daily routine.

Third and final condition—Jonathan did not want to wear a suit at the wedding. I thought that was fair. If, at eleven years of age, he was to endure the awkward exercise of observing his dad get married, no suit required! We compromised on a tucked shirt, khakis, and comfortable shoes that would allow him to play once the ceremony was over. The wedding was simple and beautiful, and Jonathan even lasted through the reception with his shirt tucked in. During our mother-son dance he looked up at me with a huge smile and chuckled. "This is weird. What should we talk about?" In those moments of our dance, we recalled our favorite parts of the *Lord of the Rings* trilogy, and you guessed it, the questions continued. It was our connection.

What I did not know then, but cherish now, is that my stepson's conditions would shape our relationship and ability to invite each other into those places of our hearts reserved for only the most special bonds. My initial anxieties about what kind of mom I would be and what it would be like to parent a preteen began to subside as I embraced the disruptive tension of the sweet, sweet invitation into Jonathan's life.

The Sweetest Invitation

It wasn't the first time my life had been disrupted by a sweet, sweet invitation. About four years prior, a friend invited me to church. I accepted the invitation with some hesitation and went to church that next Sunday. It was there that I experienced a truth that caused me, for the first time, to honestly confront my own brokenness. My encounter that day wasn't anything supremely divine. Before offering an illustration in his sermon message, the pastor turned to his wife, and with more tenderness and respect than I had ever seen between a man and woman, he sought her permission to share a personal story. The honest pause and gentle tone in his speech and softness in his eyes spoke love. It was an arguably insignificant moment that likely went unnoticed by the rest of the congregation.

Yet, it was exactly what I needed to see. That simple gesture was restorative in a way that I still don't fully understand, but it set the course for my ongoing faith journey.

Accepting the invitation from Christ that day was disruptive to be sure. I was at the beginning of my doctoral work at the time. I had built my understanding of the world on theories that had intellectual merit but very little value absent revelation of the gospel. Reevaluating my thinking and well-reasoned theories in light of the truth of Christ disoriented me at first, and I certainly did not have it all worked out by the time I defended my dissertation. It was the beginning of an ongoing process of responding to the disruptive tension of Christ's invitation to the cross found in Luke 9:23–24 ESV: "And he said to all, 'If anyone would come after me, let him deny himself and take up his cross daily and follow me. For whoever would save his life will lose it, but whoever loses his life for my sake will save it.'"

Over the years, I've come to see the Bible as a book of invitations from God. An invitation to rest, an invitation to surrender, and an invitation to become complete in Christ. Prior to accepting the invitation, we may know of a distant God. We may know of a rule-bearing religion. We may even have knowledge of biblical characters—men and women who faced temptations, who battled their own sinful nature, who rose to power and fell in the midst of their own greed and selfishness. Men and women who witnessed the miracles of Jesus on earth. But only when we step into the invitation can we experience the transformative work of the Holy Spirit, in the form of grace.

The gospel invitation to live under the lordship of Jesus is life-changing, but not without a disruptive tension. This tension is illuminated in the text of Luke 9 where believers are invited to take up their cross and be crucified, and not once, but daily. Believers are sure to experience the tension of this invitation, which paradoxically claims that life is found in death. The very tension of the gospel message is that we receive eternal, spiritual life through a God who was crucified and broken in body, and we are invited into that process.

Constructive, Nonviolent Tension

I am not the first to make a connection between tension and growth as necessary to the work of racial healing and restoration.[1] In his life, work, and death, Dr. Martin Luther King Jr. left a legacy of courage and hope and lessons about resistance and change that still deserve our close attention. To understand the entirety of Dr. King's work is to know that Dr. King was nonviolent but defiant in the face of injustice. King understood that lasting social change emerges from the disruptive, catalytic moments that unveil the hypocrisy and moral bankruptcy of established laws and norms effacing the dignity and rights of individuals.

As our nation pauses each year to reflect on the historical importance of Dr. King's work and the broader significance of the civil rights movement, I find myself returning to an article I read some years ago. The authors of the article challenged readers to ask how our public discourse around racial justice might be shaped differently if the annual commemoration of Dr. King took place on April 4 rather than January 15. That is, what if we drew our attention to Dr. King's death and the sobering reminder that he was assassinated while fighting for a ten-cent increase for sanitation workers, rather than celebrating his birth and our declared wins in the civil rights movement?[2]

The authors suggest that perhaps the recognition of King's birthday has caused us to prematurely take a victory lap in the fight toward human rights and a recognition of the full dignity of all people. But what if we were to examine the full context in which Dr. King's dream was cut short? The authors ask readers what our celebration of the civil rights leader on January 15 says about our own obsessive interest in applauding a safe Dr. King rather than responding to his more radical call to the redistribution of political and economic power. Perhaps an April holiday would remind us that even a celebrated, safe King was threatening to an

---

1. A portion of this chapter was recorded for Seattle Pacific University's Martin Luther King Jr. Chapel Service in 2018.
2. Inwood and Alderman, "What If the MLK Holiday."

established order. Our fogged, rearview-mirror-reading of history might cause us to cling nostalgically to Dr. King's "I Have a Dream" speech, but an April commemoration might prompt us to return more frequently to his "Letter from Birmingham City Jail," where King responded to critiques from White clergy who felt his protest disrupted existing peace. King was never deterred by these critiques. His social movement was nonviolent, yes, but it was never intended to be comfortable. Protest is meant to cause tension; it is an act of bearing witness to a human yearning for freedom. In his "Letter from Birmingham City Jail," Dr. King shared these words:

> But I must confess that I am not afraid of the word "tension." I have earnestly opposed violent tension, but there is a type of constructive, nonviolent tension which is necessary for growth. Just as Socrates felt that it was necessary to create a tension in the mind so that individuals could rise from the bondage of myths and half-truths to the unfettered realm of creative analysis and objective appraisal, we must see the need for nonviolent gadflies to create the kind of tension in society that will help [people] rise from the dark depths of prejudice and racism to the majestic heights of understanding and brotherhood.[3]

I continue to be struck by Dr. King's words and cannot help but pause on his use of the word *tension*—this idea that disruption is needed for change, that perhaps we must embrace disruptive tension as an essential part of transformative growth.

"The Angel with the Flaming Sword"

As someone who has been involved in diversity and racial reconciliation efforts, I have approached this work as a ministry of healing. This statement might raise eyebrows, given the many ways diversity work has been construed and misconstrued. So, I want to be very clear about what I mean by a *ministry of healing*. I often describe diversity and racial reconciliation work on two

---

3. King, "Letter from Birmingham Jail," 291.

levels. At an individual level, it is about healing distortions in our understanding of God-initiated diversity and learning to see each other as God's image bearers. Our responsibility at this level is to become aware of the hidden assumptions that limit our vision of each other as well as our actions that maintain racial hierarchies. At an institutional level, it's about alleviating historically rooted barriers to achieving wholeness.

When I work with organizations, my goal is to invite members into a conversation that will prompt movement at both levels. As one of my colleagues in this work explains, "The starting point for this work is not numbers. The starting point is human dignity."[4] The goal is to see God more clearly and to confront behaviors, words, actions, and systems that are counterproductive to God's intent for human flourishing. This is the work of diversity and racial reconciliation as a ministry of healing that can help us guard and battle against disunity.

In my ongoing efforts toward racial healing and understanding, I gain new insights into the nonviolent yet disruptive tensions that are often at the center of this work. What I love and hate most about racial reconciliation ministry work is that it completely turns me inside out. I am often challenged in a conversation, in a decision, in a moment where I am faced with my own limitations. Often, it is my desperate yearning to see the racial and cultural alienation in our world dissipate that, strangely enough, blinds me to the very person standing in front of me. My hope in this work rests not in my capacity but in my complete awe of God. In this work I see the heart of God through my shortcomings and discover my great need for him as I pursue healing across racial and cultural divides.

I stepped into the work of racial reconciliation for one reason—I felt called to it. But calling is not always enough to sustain us through the difficulties. What keeps me going is the remembrance of my alienation from Christ, the gift of his sweet, sweet

---

4. Daniel Hill (founder, River City Community Church, Chicago), special session with senior leadership team, Seattle Pacific University, January 30, 2019.

Embrace Disruptive Tensions

invitation, and the amazing realization that in the work of diversity and unity, I have an opportunity to invite others, and hopefully in a way that extends the grace so freely given to me.

I truly believe that diversity and reconciliation work is patterned after the spiritual process of salvation. Just as the invitation to salvation necessitates that we address those very areas of sin and woundedness that would keep us separated from God, so too, the invitation to living in a community of difference demands that we address those areas of woundedness that would create fractures, separation, isolation, and fear. Much like reconciliation to Christ necessitates that we understand the biblical narrative of creation and fall, our reconciliation to each other across social divides requires that we engage honestly with our cultural narratives. In the same way that our salvation requires God's grace, our diversity journey necessitates forgiveness. Each act of forgiveness moves us in the direction of God's love and closer to the kingdom-intent for diversity. In all things, the cross mediates between the perfect love of God and our fallen human condition. And it all begins with an invitation—a sweet, sweet invitation to Christ's salvific work.

What strikes me more than anything, what makes this invitation all the sweeter, is that Christ does not *need* us to fulfill the promises of the gospel. We know that the redemptive work of the cross has already been accomplished. Why, then, are we invited to be co-laborers with Christ? Why are we asked to pick up our cross? If, in fact, Christ can work independent of us, it seems, this invitation is purely God's loving reminder that we are among the called and forgiven and part of the divine creation story. This sweet, sweet invitation fraught with tension reorients us to the cross, allowing us to see our own brokenness and motivating us to be givers of the grace we received. It is in this invitation that we develop a deep awareness of Christ's presence. It is in this invitation, with the ability to respond, that we exercise our muscles to surrender.

Jesus makes clear that a decision to respond with "yes" means taking up our crosses. It is a daily posture and response of the heart, a minute-by-minute decision about who sits on the throne of our lives. Howard Thurman, the influential theologian and mentor to

Dr. King, writes that we all have an inner authority that directs our lives. In a short excerpt from his book *Meditations of the Heart*, Thurman shares these words:

> There is in every person an inward sea, and in that sea there is an island and on that island there is an altar and standing guard before that altar is the "angel with the flaming sword." Nothing can get by that angel to be placed upon that altar unless it has the mark of your inner authority. Nothing passes "the angel with the flaming sword" to be placed upon your altar unless it be a part of "the fluid area of your consent." This is your crucial link with the Eternal.[5]

The Throne of God

In the divine invitation to join Christ as co-laborers, our response is ultimately a decision about who will sit on the throne. The invitation includes a disruptive tension, for sure, as we learn to unseat ourselves from that throne. But it is also accompanied by the divine gift of entering God's reconciling mission.

- Do you see the disruptive tension of God's invitations to pick up your cross as an intrusion in your life? Or do you see it as a sweet, sweet invitation to a relationship marked by total belonging and full intimacy with God?
- Where deep divisions remain in our social fabric, are you an "arbiter or distributor of grace"?[6]
- Is there anything you need to unseat from the throne of your life (pride, fear, hostility, unforgiveness) to love across the dividing lines of race?

The disruptive invitations in my life have never left me empty hearted. Don't get me wrong. It wasn't all rosy after that initial testing

---

5. Thurman, *Meditations*, 216.
6. Phrase borrowed from the title of Pastor Todd Kaunitz's May 18, 2025, sermon.

period with my soon-to-be stepson. Jonathan and I have had our moments of misunderstanding and emotional distance. But we've laughed more than we've cried and found communion of spirit far greater than anything I could have imagined as a stepmom.

What I learned then and still know about Jonathan more than twenty years later is that he is not one for surface relationships. He seeks deep engagement, meaningful conversations, and a love that will be sustained. What I appreciate now as one of the greatest gifts I've ever received was his willingness to invite me to the most precious areas of his life, to join in his personal story and history, to embrace the things that mattered most to him, to gain insight to the way he sees the world, to enter into his pain and loss, and to empty myself in order to make room for him. Those moments of surrender to Jonathan's relational conditions make way for other similar postures in my life.

I now look back at those early days of stepping into motherhood and smile as I think about the ways Jonathan and I have grown together over the years. The disruptive tension of a sweet, sweet invitation from that eleven-year-old boy who loved his puppy, who often escaped into the world of *Lord of the Rings*, and who danced with a smile on my wedding day is a tangible reminder of Christ's invitation to genuine fellowship.

May we continue in our walk toward unity. May we grow in love as we embrace the challenge offered in Dr. King's invitation to a transformative tension that leads to radical relationships marked by shalom. May we walk in the power of Christ's redemptive glory. In all things, we can allow our human divisions to break us, or we can allow them to break us open and reveal a wholeness that God intends for his creation.[7] My son taught me that.

---

7. In his book *The Second Mountain*, David Brooks uses the phrase "broken open" to describe our ability to extend a capacious love as we grow through adversity and suffering.

In the temple he found those who were selling oxen and sheep and pigeons, and the money-changers sitting there. And making a whip of cords, he drove them all out of the temple, with the sheep and oxen. And he poured out the coins of the money-changers and overturned their tables. And he told those who sold the pigeons, "Take these things away; do not make my Father's house a house of trade." His disciples remembered that it was written, "Zeal for your house will consume me."

JOHN 2:14–17 ESV

Reflection Questions

1. Read John 2:14–17. What is being disrupted in this passage? What are we being invited to?

2. In his 1963 "Letter from Birmingham City Jail," Dr. Martin Luther King Jr. spoke of the necessity of "constructive, nonviolent tension" in the struggle for racial justice and equality. What did he mean by this statement? Does it still have relevance today?

3. Where has God used disruptive tensions in your life to bring about spiritual formation and relational growth?

3

Test the Strength of Your Rope

> Search me, O God, and know my heart! Try me and know my thoughts! And see if there be any grievous way in me, and lead me in the way everlasting!
>
> PSALM 139:23–24 ESV

Running to Shore

I WAS SO EXCITED. I planned the trip of a lifetime. Soon, my husband and children—then ages thirteen and sixteen—would be heading to my birth family's home country of Jamaica.

It can be an odd experience to marry into a family that has no connection to your racial or cultural identity. As a new wife and stepmom, I knew that entering their lives meant there would be no natural link to my past. The events that marked the stages of my life. The familiar images, sounds, and stories that engulfed my memories. The people who left an imprint on my heart. The places I called home long before I shared a home with them. The dreams

I fulfilled, and a few I left behind. As a new wife and stepmom, I walked to the tempo of my family-by-choice while seeking to compose a new syncopated rhythm together.

There were so many things I wanted them to know about my heritage. I also wanted our children to have a broader sense of the world, and the people in it, than what our culturally uniform bedroom community could provide. We lived in a "good" suburban Southern California community, the kind with cookie-cutter stucco homes. You can't imagine the glares we received in our neighborhood when we painted our house a bright golden beige. In a sea of muted colors, our house shone like a Las Vegas casino. It was the first time I understood there were unspoken community standards for exterior paint colors. It was a cultural awakening for me only second to learning that our neighborhood had a weed-abatement service.

Our community provided access to all the amenities one could ever need—supermarkets stocked with the freshest, brightest produce; a variety of banks; a range of medical facilities; and top-rated schools, parks, and trails. Our children could play outside without concern. We could leave our doors open for a cool breeze on a late autumn day. Our private backyard pool offered relief from the sun. On cooler nights, we could sit by our firepit and exchange laughter as our dog ran playfully about and caught the occasional marshmallow from our s'mores. Idyllic. Warm. Secure. I imagine it is what so many parents hope for their children. I did, too. But I wanted more. The kind of more that would leave them wanting less.

After much anticipation about our trip, we landed in Montego Bay at about ten o'clock in the evening. It was dark, raining heavily, and the streets were bustling, more than I had seen during any of my previous visits to Jamaica. It finally dawned on me. Despite my careful planning, I had scheduled our arrival during the weekend of Jamaica's Independence Day, perhaps the most eventful time of the year.

As we traveled from Montego Bay toward our destination in Green Island, the sounds of the city dissipated. I had purposely opted for a more remote part of the island away from the tourist hotspots. *But this remote?* As we traversed the dimly lit roads, I could tell our driver was lost and doubtful about his ability to reach our destination. The roads became desolate. The terrain shifted from paved to gravel roads. The stillness was eerie, and I was convinced the sky could not get darker without completely concealing our vision. When our driver finally asked if we were sure we had the right address, my initial excitement turned to concern. Beneath my fears, I calmly encouraged our travel-worn children to close their eyes and go to sleep. I took a moment to close my eyes, too, as I prayed for God's traveling mercies.

Without any evidence that a different course would yield a better outcome, we continued forward hoping that something would look familiar or at least suggest that we were heading in the right direction. A few indiscernible voices and sounds broke through the darkness. The first legible sound was reggae music. Soon the sounds were illuminated by the night sky. As moonlight shone through the trees, we could make out the silhouette of women in dancehall costumes. We made our way along the beach-lined boulevard to find that we were in the middle of an Independence Day extravaganza that commemorated the freedom of a people and a nation. I wish I could have paused long enough to appreciate the significance. But I continued to be distracted by our unexpected off-course excursion.

It was late, and I thought we must be nearing the end of our travels, but the next turn brought us to a secluded hill. As we topped a one-lane, in-and-out road, we encountered members of the Jamaican Constabulary armed with rifles and accompanied by canines. Although discomforting, this encounter ultimately set us on the right path. Our driver rolled down his window to ask an officer for directions. Just as I started to come down from the adrenaline rush that helped override my exhaustion, we approached our villa.

My relief was short-lived. The owners who greeted us at the gate were inebriated and provided less clarity and assurance than this stepmom needed. I panicked as I thought about the sensationalized, but not wholly inaccurate, stories our kids would share with their birth mom when they returned home. I wondered if we would lose custody. At a minimum, I thought this might be the last time I would be granted permission to travel with the kids.

It was nearly midnight, so we took our room key and hunkered down for the night. My thoughts were spinning as I replayed our evening. I don't remember falling asleep. After all, I couldn't have imagined finding peace enough to rest. But I did. The next thing I remember is waking up to the flame-like embers of the sun through my half-opened eyes. The brightness was both overwhelming and inviting. It's the closest thing in nature I've witnessed to heaven meeting earth. In the truest sense, morning had wiped away the darkness of night.

It didn't take long to wake the kids. As soon as they stirred, they discovered what Jon and I had already witnessed. We were in paradise! Without hesitation, both kids leaped out of bed, grabbed their swimsuits, and greeted the morning by jumping into the water.

With white sands as soft as baby powder and azure seas with temperatures like bathwater, there is nothing like the feeling of the Caribbean Sea. Healing, pure, calm. The kids took turns jumping into the water from a low cliff that allowed them to experience the joy, wonder, and freedom of God's creation. We swam back and forth from the shore to a small rock outcropping where we could pause for breath. I don't know what brought me more joy—the smiles and laughter from my family or the fact that our sense of hope and peace had been reborn. God's mercies are indeed new each day.

With the same suddenness that ushered in our joy, I was soon jolted by the panic-stricken shouts of my daughter who was in the water and halfway between me and her father, who had already reached the rock outcropping. "Get it off of me!" she screamed. "Get it off!" Tears streamed down her face. I froze mid-stroke. I was equidistant from my daughter and the shore, and I had a choice. Before I could consciously collect my thoughts, I found myself back on dry land looking out toward my daughter who was now in her father's capable grip. I don't remember going through a series of considerations or their consequences. What I remember is a reflex determination that whatever needed to get off her did not need to be on me! I saw nothing from my location in the water. So, what kind of creature could have taken hold of her? What could be, at once, so terrifying but also invisible to the human eye? Furthermore, what was it doing to her, and what would it do to *me*? Self-preservation was my immediate default.

My foot barely had time to hit the sand before the rationalizations started to shower down like coins dropping from a winning slot machine. I could not keep up with the speed of justifications that rolled in:

It's better you did not stay in the water.

After all, you might both be in danger had you stayed. What then?

Besides, Victoria is a better swimmer than you. What if you made the situation worse with your flailing arms and labored strokes?

She was already heading in the direction of her father, and he's physically stronger and much more capable. Of what help could you have been?

As my husband came out of the water carrying Victoria, I could see the red welts left by the sting of a jellyfish. I can't describe the overwhelming guilt I felt. What kind of mother was I? Did I just lack moral fiber as a human being? Was it because I was a stepmom and had missed those crucial early parent-infant bonding experiences? Then the real punch to the gut. What would her biological mother think? What would Victoria think? Would she hate me forever?

If you had asked me just five minutes before the jellyfish attack if I would do anything for my children, I would have been emphatic and indignant in my *yes*. In a crucial moment, how could I have acted in a way that was so inconsistent with my self-declared goodness?

Seeing Peter in Ourselves

Does that sound familiar? Remember the story of Peter's denial of Jesus in the courtyard of the high priest while Jesus was on trial? How could this be? Peter was one of Jesus's closest followers. He left everything to follow Jesus (Matt 4:18–22) and vowed to never leave him (Matt 26:35). He was among the first of the disciples to recognize Jesus as the Messiah (Matt 16:16). Commissioned to preach the good news, Peter was granted the keys of the kingdom of heaven (Matt 16:16–19). Among the disciples, he was the most emphatic in his *yes*. But he also struggled with doubt and fear. In a moment of weakness as Jesus was on trial and things got real, the faithful disciple disowned Jesus to save himself.

In Peter's story, we might uncover our own betrayals. The jellyfish incident was a moment of honest confrontation with my innermost self. It drew me into close proximity with my latent fears and revealed the limits of my emphatic *yes*. It softened my heart to understanding how others too might declare love and loyalties that are unproven. I was reminded also of our proneness to implicit bias—those social stereotypes so far beyond our conscious reach we can hold to the belief that we have achieved some moral high ground in overcoming the ills of prejudice and hostility. What is likely truer is that we live such culturally distanced lives that we never enact our espoused values. We can go about our ordinary days believing in our goodness and proclaiming our Christian devotion to loving *all* people without ever demonstrating that love across racial and cultural boundaries in ways that truly affirm the dignity and humanity of all people.

One of the greatest detriments to our growth in loving God and neighbor is that we can hunker down in ideologically homogeneous enclaves that simply feed the gluttony of our self-righteousness. How much have we limited our capacity to grow in grace by not exposing our hearts to the testing that comes with engaging the cultural stranger? Perhaps many of us feel confident that we have already tested our deep convictions. But do we understand what a true test looks like? I appreciate C. S. Lewis's challenge to his readers:

Test the Strength of Your Rope

You never know how much you really believe anything until its truth or falsehood becomes a matter of life or death to you. It is easy to say you believe a rope to be strong and sound as long as you are merely using it to cord a box. But suppose you had to hang by that rope over a precipice. Wouldn't you then first discover how much you really trusted it? Only a real risk tests the reality of a belief.[1]

Putting It to the Test

Testing the strength of our ropes is an important aspect of developing the capacity to love our neighbors and restore wholeness. One of the greatest barriers to healing relationships across differences is our difficulty in holding a mirror to our thinking and behaviors. A whole part of our being can remain sequestered despite our attempt at honest self-scrutiny. I am talking about those corners of our minds and hearts that remain hidden from our view. Sadly, a sudden and disruptive event often permits us to see our inner condition. We do not typically ask for those experiences to come; we certainly do not knock on the door and invite them in. They come like nebulous jellyfish. Unexpected, quiet, stinging. They show up without warning, catching us off guard, and in our response, we reflect the truest sense of ourselves. When we have these potentially revelatory experiences, they are a gift from God. It is an opportunity to see the gap between who we are presently and who we are to become in Christ. It is a chance to see our frailty, forgo judgment, and refrain from dismissing those who offend us, knowing our own offense.

In a polarized world, we can spend so much time and expend so much energy clutching our proclaimed beliefs about any number of topics including gun violence, climate change, immigration, and election security. Yet, our beliefs may not withstand scrutiny when tested. Even when our beliefs do hold, they may need to grow as we understand the expansiveness of God's creation and his

---

1. Lewis, *Grief Observed*, 20–21.

purpose in it. The Christian life provides an opportunity to draw close to the Creator and his created beings that we may begin to see more clearly and wholly and embody the love that Christ has shown us.

One aspect of our human condition that concerns me is the narrowness of our engagement with God's created. The lasting effects of residential segregation in our nation means that we have limited opportunities for meaningful diversity exchanges that are sustained and authentic. What might we be missing in our homogeneous living? How does it shape our understanding of God? How does it dampen our capacity for kingdom work? Entire realms of God's glory await us if we are willing to sit in the discomfort of our disagreements and test the strength of our rope while dedicating ourselves to unity.

Embracing Strangers as Teachers[2]

In his work *Learning from the Stranger*, David Smith challenges readers to avoid being locked into "very small mental horizons."[3] According to Smith, those who are committed to cultural engagement must foster an ability to learn from and relate respectfully to individuals whose life experiences differ vastly from their own. Furthermore, they must remain open to understanding the human condition from different points of view. This is active, demanding work that is necessary if we are to move beyond mere expressions of cultural tolerance toward a genuine commitment to living in unbroken wholeness among the strangers in our midst.

For the devout Christian who is fearful of venturing out and learning from cultural strangers, Smith sends a powerful reminder: "The Gospel of Christ calls us to respond not in fear and pharisaical judgment of others, but in critical attention to the planks in our own eyes, and in the loving attentiveness to our neighbor."[4]

---

2. A portion of this section is adapted from my previous work, Richards Mayo, "Where Riotous Difference," with permission.

3. Smith, *Learning from the Stranger*, 80.

4. Smith, *Learning from the Stranger*, 81.

Rather than fearing the possibility of being culturally contaminated, we must ask ourselves, "What might we miss if we fail to step outside of our familiar cultural boundaries?" I believe we miss the entirety of God's intent for humankind—to live as a community of difference, brought together as one, and sharing our unique gifts that are made available by the very nature of our difference.

Living in a world of difference yet remaining cloistered in one's familiar mental and geographic locations is like being given a beautiful diamond with many facets and choosing to simply gaze upon one. The facets of a diamond—the smooth surface areas cut and positioned at different angles—allow light to enter in and be reflected. These facets are what make the diamond both brilliant and durable. The more facets we carve into our lives, the more we can reflect God's love. Without those facets, we remain dull and unable to absorb light and reflect it to others, and our single-faceted lives can do little to illuminate truth to a wounded world. When we maintain hostility toward those whose viewpoints are different from our own, we not only dim our vision of the world, but we tear away at the fabric of God's tapestry.

Asking the Hard Questions

I invite you to consider a series of questions that remain central to my own ongoing reflection:

- Do you truly see the image of God in each person you encounter, beholding them as God's handiwork?
- Do you intentionally seek to live in unity, even when you disagree on politics and social issues? Before you answer yes, how have you tested the strength of your rope?
- How are your diversity exchanges causing you to see your true inclinations?
- Are there enough disruptive tensions and revelatory opportunities in your relationships to reveal where fissures exist in your heart and where deep divisions reside?

I don't know that we need to go to any extraordinary lengths to test the strength of our rope, but I believe we need to operate outside of the well-worn grooves of our daily lives. It may be a small change to our daily patterns, like choosing to take public transportation to work instead of driving in the comforts of our car. Doing so not only disrupts our routine, but it places us in proximity with individuals we might not otherwise encounter. A small act can open our hearts to a greater awareness of God's presence and purpose in adopting us into his diverse family.

- If you were to take stock of the people in your circle, what observations would you make as it pertains to diversity?
- As you think about your closest friends and neighbors, your coworkers, and the members of your congregation, do they share similar political affiliations, cultural identities, and backgrounds?
- Are you likely to find cohesion in your viewpoints and understanding of the world?

Building Relational Capacity

Seeking familiarity is not wrong, but it can limit our growth. If you have ever attempted to build muscle strength, you know that you have to change up parts of your workout every four to six weeks to shock your muscles and prevent adaptation. By doing so, you continually challenge your body. If we repeat the same exercises, we are prone both to more injury and to fewer gains. In physical exercise, as in most aspects of life where we seek growth, we need enough challenge and support to attain the changes we seek. Similarly, to test the strength of our rope in relationships, we need to go beyond familiar borders and step into community with the strangers in our midst.

To begin, you might think about the individuals with whom you already commune. I am not talking about the people you brush up against to and from work or while running errands. I'm not even talking about the individuals who attend the same church or workplace. We know all too well that shallow acquaintance can be the norm even in professional settings and places of worship. I am talking about the individuals with whom there is a necessity for a relationship over time, where there is a tie (legal or otherwise) that will tether you through disagreement, disappointment, and even physical distance.

As we incline our hearts toward one another, disagreements and all, we gain the capacity to see and know the One who is limitless in his love and asks us to be limitless in ours. As we test the strength of our rope and see its frayed edges, we gain capacity to see the Peter in ourselves. We discover that the same redemption made available for a disciple who betrayed Jesus is available for us. We become grateful for the sustaining grace of God that meets us even when fear causes us to run to shore. In this grace, we can meet each other at the foot of the cross, place our differences at the altar, and seek understanding and healing, knowing redemption is not our own work but God's.

Homeward

> Search me, O God, and know my heart! Try me and know my thoughts! And see if there be any grievous way in me, and lead me in the way everlasting!
>
> Psalm 139:23–24 ESV

Reflection Questions

1. Read Ps 139:23–24. What is David's prayer? How often has this been your prayer?

2. Think of a time when God revealed "any offensive way" that hindered you from loving your neighbor fully. How did you respond?

3. How might you apply Ps 139:23–24 to the commandment to "love the Lord your God with all your heart and with all your soul and with all your mind . . . and love your neighbor as yourself"?

4

Be a Salve

> I counsel you to buy from me gold refined by fire, so that
> you may be rich, and white garments so that you may clothe
> yourself and the shame of your nakedness may not be seen,
> and salve to anoint your eyes, so that you may see.
>
> REVELATION 3:18 ESV

Reflections on Race[1]

BEING IN AN INTERRACIAL marriage sometimes means there will be difficult conversations about race. It has been no different for me and Jon. For Jon, race has been largely neutral and distant—a matter of fact, but not of consequence. For me, racial realities have been ever-present and salient, and at times searing and pungent. Race has touched every aspect of my life, leaving traces of

---

1. An earlier version of this section previously appeared as a newsletter article for the Seattle Pacific University Office of Diversity, Equity, and Inclusion in 2020. Page no longer available; copy of originals in author's possession.

its marred history on my heart. Two very different lived experiences. Two very different ways of understanding the world. Over the years, there were race conversations so difficult, it seemed ridiculous to have them. There have been times Jon asked why we needed to have them. After all, why was *I* making everything about race? I wish it were that simple.

It is difficult to put into words the subtle and not-so-subtle ways that race has shown up uninvited. When I look back on the chapters of my life, race is always there, defining, shaping, and reshaping the dynamics of ordinary relationships and experiences. Most of the time race has not been at the forefront, so I don't want to overstate its presence. Race is more like a shadow that hovers and comes into peripheral view, exaggerating and distorting our perception. In one form or another, it has always been there.

In the fall of 1990, more than thirty years ago, I headed to Rutgers University as a college freshman. Weeks before the fall semester started, I received my housing and roommate assignment. The welcome letter shared information about orientation weekend and an encouragement for new students to call their roommates and get to know each other before arriving on campus. I remember my first conversation with my roommate. She sensed that I was different. She said she could hear it in the way I talked. "Are you Black?" she asked. "You're the first Black person I know."

I was one of two Black people on my residence hall floor that year. That was nothing new to me. I grew up in a predominantly White neighborhood. What was new to me was residing, day and night, with my White peers. What was new to me was the near-daily experience of explaining my hair routine. What was new to me was the gaze of floormates as I placed a satin scarf on my head each night. The questions drained me, not because curiosity is inherently invasive, but because the inquisitiveness often carried racial judgment.

I was ten when I learned that race matters. We were preparing to read a passage about the Underground Railroad. My teacher asked if I could stand up and tell the class about the Underground Railroad because, in his words, "After all, those are your kind of people." I didn't know what that meant, but I knew from the tone of his voice there was little affection for *my kind of people*. I stood silently with a mix of shame and embarrassment until he permitted me to sit down. It was the first of many classroom experiences that left me feeling naked under the racial gaze.

In some ways, college was different. I had choices. As an English major, I could choose from a menu of literature courses. Goodbye, Herman Melville, Arthur Miller, and Charles Dickens. Hello, Nella Larsen, Claude McKay, and Langston Hughes. College was the first time I was introduced to and read a book written by a Black author. When I read the Harlem Renaissance writers, words on the page pulsated with meaning. I had no relationship to these authors, but they tapped a common experience and gave me a language for things I knew in my bones. College, or at least my classes with Professor Cheryl Wall, was different. I saw my full humanity in the pages I read.

College was also the time that I started to understand something was wrong with our criminal justice system. It was my junior year. Sitting in my dorm room one afternoon, I was startled by a commanding knock. I opened the door to two men who identified themselves as federal agents. They showed me their badges and explained they were investigating a case of scholarship fraud, and they thought I might have some information related to the case. They placed a police sketch in front of me and asked if I knew who was pictured. I didn't, but their line of questioning moved quickly from "Do you know who this is?" to "Isn't this you?" They were insistent and continued to point out the resemblance. Nothing made sense in that moment. I don't know that I've ever described the experience as racialized. I don't know that it was. The sketch was racially ambiguous at best. What I know is that by this time in my life, most things took on racial meaning.

That same year a young Black man was shot in the back by a police officer a few miles from my college campus. We marched in protest, stopping traffic on New Brunswick's Route 18. I didn't know why I was marching or if it mattered. What I know now is that I was looking for a community to help me understand matters of life and death and race. I didn't find answers then, but I certainly had questions.

Similar questions resurfaced several years after I graduated from college. I was living and working just outside of New York City. The news reported the police shooting of Amadou Diallo, a Guinean immigrant living in the Bronx. He was the victim of mistaken identity, unarmed, and fired at forty-one times by four officers while trying to enter his apartment. Forty-one shots. More than twenty-five years later, that number is still incalculable to me.

As I am writing this chapter, a conversation with my brother reminded me of how short twenty-five years is in the arc of history. It was December 2, 2023, the morning of my nephew's sixteenth birthday and the day he was scheduled to take the Scholastic Aptitude Test (SAT). On the way to the testing site, my brother stopped at the supermarket to purchase a breakfast pastry and orange juice for my nephew. While my nephew waited in the car for what should have been a quick stop, my brother was being interrogated by three police officers while shopping. "Hey, buddy," they exclaimed, as my brother paused with his items in hand. "What are you doing?" Such questions are not genuine and, therefore, don't require answers. It didn't take long for the officers to determine that my brother was not the subject of the alleged call they received.

Most days I don't recall these instances, but they hold a place in my life story. Sometimes the memories make me strong. Sometimes they make me angry. Often, they make me hyper-attuned to my environment. But always and in all ways, my memories motivate me to address how race manifests in our lives and relationships.

To anyone who asks, my response is the same: race is not something I've *tried* to make much of. It simply is, and therefore I contend. These days, rather than asking others to know the full repercussions of race for those historically positioned at the bottom of the racial hierarchy, I simply ask, "Will you be a salve?" In other words, will you join in God's redemptive work with an orientation toward bringing healing and restoration? "Will you be a salve?" is a question not of confrontation or accusation, but of invitation. It is intended to put away division and summon genuine partnership in the collective and ongoing work of racial healing. Many will argue that racial wounds should already be healed. Enough time has passed. It's time to move on. I would argue that racial progress is not the same as racial healing. Rather than simply stopping abuses, we have a kingdom responsibility to be instruments of peace and shalom. When we incline our hearts toward God in this way, we become less preoccupied with making our experience the authority for determining when someone is worthy of our understanding or compassion. Instead, we find every opportunity to be molded by God into the image of his Son—the ultimate healer and comforter.

Throughout the gospel accounts, we see that Jesus is a healer and that he heals with purpose. During his ministry on earth, Jesus steps into and redeems the stories of ordinary men and women and turns them into testimonies, as he did with Mary Magdalene (Luke 8:2). Jesus reaches out his hand and shows compassion toward the man with leprosy (Luke 5:12–16). He consoles and attends to the suffering of the afflicted, as in the story of the woman who bled for twelve years (Luke 8:43–48). Jesus heals to bring glory to the Father, as in raising Lazarus from the dead (John 11:38–44). In his ultimate act, Jesus died on the cross to restore our relationship with God. This is our model for living as heaven-bound healers preparing for our eternal home—healers who can step into one other's stories, reach out in compassion, and attend to suffering in a way that exalts God's name.

Redemption and Hope

The story of Mary Magdalene is one of my favorite biblical stories of healing, although we know very little about this biblical figure. We first learn of Mary in the Gospel of Luke. We know that she was a sinful woman, broken in spirit. We know that she was under the control of seven demons. We don't know the nature of her condition or infirmity, but we know that Jesus set her free. Although he was aware of her sins, he did not reject or abandon her. Instead, he stepped into her story—in all the brokenness and despair—and redeemed it, doing so against all social norms that would relegate a woman with an unsavory reputation to an outcast. Jesus's divine love and compassion reached across such boundaries and restrictions bringing about one of the most powerful testimonies.

Mary not only becomes a devoted follower of Jesus, but she also becomes an eyewitness to Jesus's crucifixion and resurrection, and in no small way. Mary is not a footnote to these historical accounts. Instead, she becomes a central character. In John 19:25, Mary stands at the cross of Jesus along with his mother and his mother's sister—the most central women in his life. She witnesses the final moments of Jesus's life on earth as darkness comes over the whole land and Jesus cries out and breathes his last breath (Mark 15:33–41). Along with his mother, Mary observes as Jesus is laid in the tomb the day before the Sabbath (Mark 15:46–47). Mary also returns when the Sabbath has passed, bringing spices to anoint his body only to discover that the stone had been rolled away from the tomb and that Jesus had risen (Mark 16:1–6). Mary is also the first to whom Jesus appears after his resurrection (Mark 16:9).

While Scripture doesn't tell us for sure why Mary was chosen to bear witness to these events, which had been prophesied throughout the Old Testament, we can imagine it had something to do with her devotion. Mary had proven to be a faithful witness who shared about Jesus's good works. Who better to serve as a messenger of hope and healing than a woman who had no hope and was overcome by the power of Jesus, redeemed in her own brokenness and despair, something that could only be accomplished through the one true Messiah.

When Mary sees the risen Jesus, he instructs her to tell the disciples that he will be ascending to the Father, demonstrating his victory over death. This is perhaps the most important message Jesus can deliver in the culmination of his mission, and he entrusts Mary to deliver it. As Jesus's atoning sacrifice is completed, the disciples will no longer be in his earthly presence. Instead, they will receive the gift of his Holy Spirit, the Comforter (John 14:26). What begins as a story of Jesus stepping into the life of a woman tormented by seven demons ends with a testimony of a faithful

BE A SALVE

follower, healed by the Savior, and empowered to be a messenger of the Good News. This is no accident of Jesus's ministry.

When Jesus steps into our lives, he brings restoration. As we are transformed by his Spirit, we embrace the opportunity to step into someone else's pain and become a vessel for healing. As we navigate barriers of difference and "get proximate to suffering," we develop an empathy and compassion that allows for the perfect exchange of love—from Father to Son and Holy Spirit and outward.[2] As we learn to listen well across fault lines, we discover our common humanity and find we are no longer attuned simply to the words of the speaker. It is in the cracks and fissures that we find a way to reach in and through the brokenness of our human condition by listening with an intent to bring healing. This ability to listen deeply is a posture we can develop and hone through a life of genuine fellowship that rightly places Christ at the center as both our means and end.

In his classic work *Life Together*, Dietrich Bonhoeffer spoke of the necessity of listening as an essential part of Christian fellowship:

> Many people are looking for an ear that will listen. They do not find it among Christians, because these Christians are talking where they should be listening. But he who can no longer listen to his brother will soon be no longer listening to God either; he will be doing nothing but prattle in the presence of God too. This is the beginning of the death of the spiritual life, and in the end there is nothing left but spiritual chatter and clerical condescension arrayed into pious words.[3]

I would argue that this kind of listening, this kind of healing, isn't just about individuals and relationships. It's also about the institutions and structures that shape our lives.

---

2. Bryan Stevenson, civil rights attorney and founder of the Equal Justice Initiative, is credited with coining the phrase "getting proximate to suffering." Stevenson reminds us that social change begins with the empathy and understanding that develops as we draw close to the suffering of those who have been excluded.

3. Bonhoeffer, *Life Together*, 97–98.

Homeward

Hand-Me-Downs and Mending Our Societal Fabric

Even as a child, my sister was a connoisseur of all things beauty and fashion. Her sense of style was complete—hair, outfit, shoes, and accessories—all coordinated with sophistication. We grew up during the 1980s when shoulder pads, bright-colored earrings, and long faux-pearl necklaces were in. Leave it to my sister to take it to the next level with high heels and wide fashion belts to finish her look. Don't get me wrong, I had nice clothes too. But my look was more utilitarian. Even nice clothes looked sort of basic on me. I was a bit lanky—not especially tall, but my legs were long and skinny.

As a young girl, I would sneak into my sister's closet to admire her wardrobe. I would dream of borrowing something—a little something like that lavender and pink jumpsuit with puffy sleeves, a belted waist, and buttons down the back. Getting the chance to wear it while it was still in my sister's possession was unlikely. So, I set my eyes on the day she would outgrow or lose interest in it.

I loved hand-me-downs because I admired the one who handed them down. I even wanted my hair to look like my sister's. At the age of twelve, I started getting relaxers. No more pigtails. I could wear my hair with style, or so I thought. I learned to blow dry and curl it, watching my sister's every move. Yet, no matter how hard I tried, my hair never turned out like hers. Entire sections resisted holding a curl, while other parts were too curly or frizzy. Any breeze or swift movement could send my hair into a static frenzy. Even my bangs waved above my head like a flag of surrender alerting me to my hair defeat. The rest of my hair followed in rebellious independence. Neither mousse nor gel could tame the beast that was my hair.

Still, I kept trying to achieve my sister's look. If I couldn't match her hair, at least I could wear her gently worn clothes. But there was another hurdle to overcome. My sister and I had different proportions. Not drastically so, but enough that the hand-me-downs were never as flattering on me. My long legs made pants problematic. Even my mom's best alterations couldn't overcome the unwanted gap between the hem and my shoes. To conceal the breach, I would sit with my legs extended outward under my desk. And so was my childhood—stitched together with hand-me-down hopes.

As an adult, I have found the concept of hand-me-downs to be a helpful metaphor for how racial minorities often experience ordinary life within institutions that were not created with them in mind. While laws, policies, and even attitudes have changed resulting in greater access and opportunity, often the very fabric of schools and workplaces holds their original design. Continued alterations, no matter how well-executed, fail to create the kind of fit that might be possible had the original pattern considered the various dimensions of our nation's diversity. For racial minorities, the hand-me-downs continue to be ill-fitted, no matter how many adjustments they make, while majority culture individuals wonder why members of historically marginalized groups just won't assimilate. This dynamic is one of many that remains at the heart of racial misunderstanding, stereotyping, and animosity.

It will take spiritual eyes to see the ways in which our institutions and relationships hold their racial past. It will take the heart of God to move us in the direction of healing and restoration. Together we can fashion a garment suitable for all, but we cannot do so by simply sewing a new piece of cloth onto the old (Mark 2:21–22). We must become a new creation, formed as a dwelling place for the Holy Spirit, transformed into a people whose desire is to bring healing and wholeness.

A Healed Vision

The pursuit of reconciliation requires that we pause long enough to listen well, to seek understanding without judgment or condemnation, and to steward the gift of grace, freely and fully. Furthermore, it necessitates both relational and structural repair.

As we traverse social fractures and divisions, we hold the capacity to be the Balm in Gilead we all need. Yet, there is more to bringing healing than simply stepping in and attending to the areas of division and brokenness left by the original sin that separated us from God. The beginning of healing is actually salvation by faith, which requires revelation. In Rev 3:18 ESV, Jesus instructs the church of Laodicea to buy from him, "salve to anoint [their] eyes so that [they] may see." Metaphorically, Jesus was referring to an eye ointment that would bring spiritual illumination or clear understanding of the gospel. Although wealthy from a carnal perspective, the church of Laodicea had embraced false doctrines and was unwilling to repent. They were spiritually poor and blind to it.

Scripture reveals a strong connection between our posture toward repentance and our ability to see with spiritual perception. Jesus came into this world to bring sight to those whose hearts are open to God's revelatory truth (John 9:39). Jesus was also clear that he would bring blindness to those who already have sight—those who lean on their own understanding and self-sufficiency and are unwilling to repent. Matthew 13:15 (ESV) is the fulfillment of a prophecy from Isaiah, where Jesus foretold that judgment would fall upon the people of Israel and Judah for their rebellion. It is also a warning to us today about the consequences of an unrepentant heart:

> For this people's heart has grown dull, and with their ears they can barely hear, and their eyes they have closed, lest they should see with their eyes and hear with their ears and understand with their heart and turn, and I would heal them.

An unrepentant heart is dangerous because it rejects the grace of God and dampens our senses to the Holy Spirit.

I've come to believe that race and racism are spiritual sins that begin with a denial of the image of God in another person and flourish in an atmosphere where repentance cannot be found. This sinfulness is a malady not simply of our eyes, but of our hearts. As a nation, we've attempted to navigate the sins of race and racism through constitutional amendments, legislation, violent and nonviolent resistance, political and cultural maneuvers, and appeals to moral values and civic virtues, all of which have brought progress. Yet hostilities remain, divisions persist, misunderstandings prevail, and healing awaits. We fail to speak about our legacy of race without collapsing into blame or shame, or worse yet, denial. We struggle with honesty in our historical accounting. We continually turn the page without inviting God into the messiness of our story. Our actions suggest we prefer to move on rather than confess and await as the holy grace of God unfolds. All the while, our spiritual blindness prevents us from seeing both the truth of our racial condition and the need for a healing ointment or salve.

The very thing we need is the very thing Jesus can provide. There is no limit to Jesus's healing mission because healing is part of redemption, and it's something we get to participate in. This promise should excite us and bring hope to the places we inhabit relationally and physically.

HOMEWARD

I counsel you to buy from me gold refined by fire, so that you may be rich, and white garments so that you may clothe yourself and the shame of your nakedness may not be seen, and salve to anoint your eyes, so that you may see.

REVELATION 3:18 ESV

Reflection Questions

1. Read Rev 3:18. What is the significance of this passage to Christ's healing mission? What does it require of us?
2. What is your favorite story of healing in Scripture, and what does it reveal about the divine nature of God?
3. Reconciliation requires seeing each other as God sees us, as bearers of his image worthy of love and dignity. What are some of the cultural and historical factors that limit our capacity to see ourselves and each other as God sees us?

5

Share History, Share His Story

> You are witnesses of these things.
>
> LUKE 24:48 ESV

Sidewalk Joys

I REMEMBER THE SIDEWALKS in my childhood neighborhood well. While the street presented an almost certain danger, the sidewalk was that space in between—beyond the immediate protections and supervision of home, yet safe enough that we could test the margins of life without any considerable risk.

The sidewalks created a stretch of open space for adventures of all variety. My siblings and I would roller-skate down our driveway as it sloped onto the sidewalk. Avoiding small twigs and rocks and navigating the different concrete surfaces, some pebbled and some smooth, was part of the challenge and fun. I was particularly fond of the tarred-over cracked areas. Those sticky black surfaces created the optimal roller-skating conditions—quiet, effortless, and smooth.

Homeward

We spent our summer days riding bikes back and forth on the sidewalk. Sometimes my brother and I shared a single bike. One of us would be the driver. The other would be the passenger seated on the lower bar carrying all the equipment we needed—kickball, Wiffle ball and bat, and of course, a pair of roller skates.

We never ran out of good ideas. One September day, my brother and I decided to purchase a birthday cake for our mom. We had such high hopes! At first, we called the bakery to see if they could deliver it. The bakery staff met our childhood naivete with a gentle response letting us know they only delivered large cakes. We quickly gathered our thoughts, counted our change and dollar bills, shoved them into our pockets, and hopped on our bikes. This was the biggest surprise we had ever planned, and the excitement fueled our legs as we kicked our pedals into gear.

When we arrived, there were so many beautiful pastries behind the glass case to choose from. Our eyes grew large, and our hearts beat fast as we considered the many options and which one would bring the greatest delight to our mom. As we pulled out our small savings, the lady behind the counter helped us narrow our choices. Watching her place the floral-decorated lemon-filled vanilla cake into the box and secure it with that special baker's red and white twine made it all worth the effort. We had done something spectacular, and we could not wait to surprise our mom. We jumped on our bikes and secured the cake box on my handlebar. We never even considered how the undulating sidewalk might affect the cake. Despite the loss of icing on at least one side of the cake, that day we knew we had used our bikes for good and the sidewalks had served us well.

That was not always the case. Some days there was more mischief than good. Against our mother's warning, we would often race our bikes on the sidewalks. This defiance went mostly unnoticed until one time my front tire hit a protruding curbstone and sent me diving headfirst over my handlebars. While I remained conscious, the landing knocked the wind out of me. My terrified brother ran home only to announce that I was dead. I can only imagine what my dear mother prepared herself to find at the scene.

Share History, Share His Story

Fortunately, she did not have to see me sprawled on my back. After the initial shock, I picked myself up and journeyed home on foot, broken body and bike in tow. As I walked toward my mom and brother, the bitterness of my disobedience and the impending consequences sunk in.

Sometimes racing on the sidewalk was a matter of necessity, like when a neighborhood dog got loose. Nothing converts a Huffy bike into a supercharged engine like the sound of a gnarling dog at your heels.

All in all, the sidewalk was a natural runway for our childhood antics, the place where we could run and play with a sense of abandon. We also etched tracks on our sidewalks with our daily journey to school, to the playground, to the homes of other neighborhood children, and to the corner store where we could purchase Lemonheads for a dime.

The sidewalk was where we waited for the bus as we journeyed to the public library, local shopping centers, or doctor's office. As we watched impatiently for the bus while bracing the Northeast winters, the sidewalk created a horizon upon which we could set our eyes and look toward our destination with anticipation. The sidewalk contoured our vision, creating the bridge between our current space and foreseeable future. Cracks on the sidewalk reminded us that cold winters had come and gone. Raised concrete drew our attention to the tree roots growing underneath the pavement and warned of trip hazards. The cracks and raised concrete also set off our imaginations as we envisioned an intricate underground railway for ants to travel to sources of food and water. During the winter months those same sidewalks opened an avenue for childhood entrepreneurship, as my brother and I earned money and the admiration of our adult neighbors as we shoveled snow.

The sidewalk was the place where we marked our days step by step and inched toward our tomorrows. My childhood memory of the sidewalks as cherished communal space sharply contrasts what I now understand to be troubled ground where rights and access have not always been freely or equally granted. A place of negotiated tensions, legal restriction, and unspoken codes of conduct. A place where racial stereotypes have often defined who is considered safe and who poses a threat, as well as who belongs and who does not.

Sidewalk Etiquette

Some years ago, while at a park in my Southern California suburb neighborhood, I overheard a group of women relaying the events of their morning. Although not directly involved in the conversation, I listened intently as one woman explained that a house alarm had been triggered in the area. This statement was immediately followed by her recollection that she had seen a group of young Black males in the neighborhood that morning. As the conversation progressed, she came to three well-articulated, yet unfounded conclusions. One, the house alarm signaled that there had been a crime or attempted crime. Two, there was a group of young Black males walking in the neighborhood, which was worth mentioning. Three, the Black males were likely involved in the events that activated the alarm. The very presence of the young Black males raised enough suspicion that she either did not remember seeing any White people walking in the neighborhood that morning, or she found their presence so inconsequential it was not worth mentioning. I imagine the woman I encountered that morning was simply recounting her experience without knowing she was actually reciting one of our nation's dominant racial narratives.

The practice of monitoring and regulating public space is not new in the United States. During the period of chattel slavery, laws regulated the behavior of free and enslaved Black Americans in shared public space. Black individuals could not leave their masters' plantation without having written permission, and enslaved and freed Black Americans could not convene for social activity or gather for prayer or worship.

Following the Civil War, similar restrictions existed in the American South. Black Codes were instituted to restrict the rights of newly freed people to access public spaces. Jim Crow laws, which lasted for about one hundred years through the mid-twentieth century, reinforced the idea that for Black Americans, every aspect of shared public life was to be controlled and restricted. In the racial caste system of Jim Crow society, signs clearly demarcated facilities reserved for White individuals and those relegated to Black people. Jim Crow etiquette further dictated the norms by which Black and White Americans should address each other, with Black people consigned to the humiliation of inferiority in all aspects of engagement.

In Southern states, local customs limited the extent to which Black people could move freely through public space. For instance, Black people were expected to step off the sidewalk or walk in the street when encountering a White person. Violations of Jim Crow law resulted in legal lynchings and other forms of violence to regulate the behavior of Black people. Even with the elimination of legal discriminatory practices, historical inertia makes it difficult to stop the force of time-hallowed racial postures, assumptions, and fears that play out in public spaces, including sidewalks.

While sidewalks are used primarily for movement from one location to another, they are more than that. Sidewalks play a role in enabling interaction among and between individuals and with the natural world, our environment. Sidewalks are spaces that connect the private sphere to the communal, where neighborhoods flourish and cities come alive.

Racialized Terrain

When my brother and I were children, we journeyed along our sidewalks with a sense of freedom and enthusiasm. Yet, somewhere between the innocence of childhood and prudence of adulthood, the hidden contours of the past became visible.

What I had been taught and believed was that the civil rights movement eliminated the need for concern about racial matters. As I entered my early adult years and experienced life beyond the sanitized histories taught in school, I noticed a strange disconnect. The textbook depiction of race in the United States was oddly

Homeward

silent on the cascading effects of racial hostility. This gap became even more apparent as I witnessed my brother's experiences.

I am aware that as a Black man my brother continues to experience the humiliation of race as caste. I remember the first time he visited me at the university where I was pursuing my postgraduate studies. I was showing him around campus, when suddenly we were stopped by a campus safety officer who asked if everything was okay. Reflexively, we replied, "Yes." Our brain was doing something for us our mouths were not fully prepared to articulate. Before we could process why we were being stopped, we were asked to present our IDs. We complied. After a cursory check, the officer handed our IDs back to us and explained that someone had called because they saw something suspicious. It is a strange experience to know that in the simple act of navigating public space you might be considered out of place. No one ever tells you that you are being stopped because of your race. Instead, you are left to wonder and examine in the isolation of your own mind. It is a cruel mental project.

Years after that incident, my brother confided that during his morning walks he often encountered women crossing the street or clutching their handbag out of distrust. These occurrences became so commonplace that he has chosen to walk in the street. To preserve the "safety" of others and shield himself from the hurtful gestures of those who perceived him as a threat, my brother relinquished his rights to the public sidewalks. My brother's experience upon those unassuming slabs of concrete illuminate for me the ways sidewalks have always functioned not only as a conduit to people and places, but as a regulatory space defining who belongs.

I no longer look at the sidewalk simply as a place to run with a sense of childlike adventure. I am an adult, after all, and I see sidewalks, neighborhoods, and cities in all their complexity. These are racialized topographies—not in totality but in good measure.

Share History, Share His Story

Contested Space[1]

When Jon and I moved from Southern California to Seattle in 2015, two things were immediately evident. The first was visually stunning and discernible. Lush plants and vibrant moss carpeting every outdoor surface signaled that Seattle had rightfully earned its nickname as the Emerald City. As we walked along the beach in West Seattle's Lincoln Park for the very first time, we became acutely aware of our smallness in contrast to the grandeur of the Puget Sound to our left and towering evergreens to our right. This is the part of the Pacific Northwest that beckoned us: a physical landscape of transcendent beauty.

The second was obscure but staggering. In the process of purchasing our new home, our realtor directed our attention to a singular, historical clause embedded in our housing deed packet:

> Tracts or parcels of land in this plot shall be used or occupied only by persons of the White or Caucasian race and no other persons shall be permitted to use or occupy said tracts or parcels except employees may occupy the premises where their employer resides.[2]

This single phrase, dated July 1, 1946, is part of a larger body of zoning ordinances that enforced neighborhood segregation in Seattle until 1968 when the Fair Housing Act was signed into law. Racially restrictive covenants like the one attached to our home's original deed are no longer legally enforceable yet still shape national housing and economic landscapes. It came as no surprise that our neighborhood in Seattle was demographically homogeneous reflecting its deliberate construction. This is the part of the Pacific Northwest that apprehended us: a physical landscape of transcendent brokenness.

Both Seattle artifacts provided signposts to the city's local history and context. The green spaces reminded us of the visible elements of God-given diversity; the built spaces reminded us of

---

1. This section is reproduced from my earlier work, Richards Mayo, "Know Urban History's Impact," with permission.
2. Joslin et al., *Restrictions Covering Plat of Arroyo Vista*, 444.

inequities in human design. The juxtaposition between Seattle's parks and waterfront and its racially segregated built spaces is reflective of the fracture between God's perfect creation and humankind's fallen nature. Our sidewalks, neighborhoods, and cities should be places of radical belonging. Jesus's atoning death on the cross brought death to the kind of hostility that would leave lasting divisions. Yet, we are living in the already and not-yet kingdom of God, and historical divisions persist. There are traces of our history everywhere, and it matters.

Contested Histories

Those engaged in the work of racial reconciliation and healing know the difficulty in reaching agreement about our nation's historical past. The historical narratives we inherit have been filtered through the lens of those who record them, leaving a tapestry of half-truths and redacted memories. Even when there is a reasonable consensus, a partial retelling of those events left unquestioned can distort our sense of time, impact, and magnitude. Using the civil rights movement as an example, criminal justice attorney Bryan Stevenson has this to say:

> I hear people talking about the civil rights movement and it sounds like a three-day carnival. On day one, Rosa Parks did not give up her seat on the bus. On day two, Martin Luther King led a march in Washington. And on day three, we just changed all the laws."[3]

Given this common chronological depiction, our nation's racial problems can be misconstrued as ephemeral and readily uprooted by laws.

Yet, this script runs counter to the experiences of historically marginalized groups who continue to experience the long-standing effects of racism in the United States. For Black Americans, the civil rights era is not simply a period of discriminatory acts followed by a series of victories. Instead, the freedom struggle

---

3. Wong, "Bryan Stevenson Highlights Racism," para. 15.

Share History, Share His Story

is ongoing and marked by historical acts—like the 1955 murder of Emmett Till—that resonate with current-day race relations. Others have drawn parallels between the killings of Emmett Till, Trayvon Martin, and Ahmaud Arbery, illuminating patterns of surveillance and violence that have survived the implementation of civil rights laws.[4] Even when old laws are abolished and new laws are passed, historical inertia exerts a force that seems unstoppable. In all three cases, the victim was a young Black male. In all three cases, the victim was perceived to be a threat based on unsubstantiated claims. In all three cases, the young males died before they could share their side of the story. All three killings, which stretch over a period of sixty-five years, took place despite civil rights gains. And, while history purports to be the past, the loss of these young lives—ages fourteen, seventeen, and twenty-five, respectively—tells a different story. As James Baldwin notes, "History is not the past. It is our present. We carry our history with us. We are our history."[5]

Those whose bodies hold the traces of entrenched societal pathologies continue to bear their metastatic patterns. Those whose bodies have not been host to the horrors of racial terror and its companion evils may not detect the prevalence of latent and active malignancies. As people of different hues, we walk through life historically distanced from one another and lacking a "common memory" that can unite us in genuine fellowship formed in truth and love and enacted in justice and mercy.[6] Current executive initiatives to recast our national history can deepen the divide and have corrosive consequences for what it means to share in communal life.[7] How we choose to vote, our decisions about what regions of the country we live, and even our ecclesial affiliations

---

4. See, for example, Bey, "'Bring Out Your Dead'"; and Onwuachi-Willig, "Policing the Boundaries."

5. Quoted in Peck, *I Am Not Your Negro*.

6. I first learned the phrase "common memory" from Mark Charles, a speaker, consultant, and coauthor of the book *Unsettling Truths*.

7. Refers to Executive Order No. 14253, *Restoring Truth and Sanity to American History*.

are born, in part, out of our historical memories. For much of my life, I avoided visiting the Southern states and swore I would never live below the Mason–Dixon line. My understanding of how slavery shaped the Confederate states caused my aversion to life in the South. I know I am not alone in the ways in which a racialized history has informed my experiences and choices.

The Hope of a Redeemed History

How, then, do we overcome this dilemma? If we truly experience life from different vantage points, is unity possible? I believe it is, but we must correctly diagnose the problem. We must bring a remedy to the incomplete stories we have been told and the resulting assumptions that shape our perception. In other words, we must learn the whole story before drawing conclusions about the world. According to Bryan Stevenson, the challenge before us is a narrative one.

As we endeavor toward unity and unbroken wholeness, we must confront our human story, honestly, thoroughly, and courageously. But what does it mean to face history courageously? I believe there are at least four requisite elements: humility, lament, repentance, and repair.

Humility

We can never rewrite the past in its entirety as a perfectly recorded set of chronological events. Rather, we must appreciate history as a process in which individuals create and recreate the past by drawing on available source material. These sources are always partial and incomplete and, as such, can never fully represent the events exactly as they occurred. In this state of unknowing, we can humbly acknowledge that all human knowledge is limited and that wisdom comes from God. From a posture of humility, we can seek to understand the totality of the human experience by broadening the scope of historical narratives that are collected and preserved. In so doing, we can establish a common memory that leads to healing.

Lament

Part of the work in creating a common memory is learning to embrace the role of biblical lament. In his exploration of the book of Lamentations, Soong-Chan Rah examines the historical significance of lament over the fall of Jerusalem and calls on Christians today to reclaim this spiritual practice as an active and communal response to suffering. According to Rah, biblical lament "recounts historical suffering"[8] and "allows for honesty before God and each other."[9] It is an expression of solidarity in burden-bearing. Even when we do not understand the weight of history another might experience, our devotion to Christian fellowship should cause us to grieve our inability to relate to the other's suffering and to seek the Holy Spirit's help in understanding.

Repentance

Lament brings us to communal repentance and offers a way to redemption through Jesus Christ. As we recognize and face our inherited and shared responsibility in the world's brokenness, we can face history honestly, freely confess our national sins and their consequences, and seek God's healing and deliverance from the bondage of our past. Only through genuine repentance can we experience freedom through Christ and see the rule of God in our midst as we seek unity across differences.

Repair

I no longer speak about reconciliation and unity across differences without also talking about repair. I realize the topic of reparations is divisive. So often the discussion devolves into debates about whether there should be monetary compensation given to the descendants of enslaved Africans and other groups that still bear the

---

8. Rah, *Prophetic Lament*, 44.
9. Rah, *Prophetic Lament*, 47.

burdens of racial inequities set in motion centuries ago. It is difficult to get beyond the debates and to move toward meaningful dialogue. But, as the body of Christ, we miss an important component of reconciliation if we are not actively working toward repair—in all forms. The question before the church is not *can we achieve true justice and repair?* Instead, we must ask, *is our heart inclined toward that pursuit?* Furthermore, when it comes to sharing our national history, do we seek to be transformed by the gospel?

There is healing to be found in our history. We can be certain of this because of his story. Jesus came to fulfill the Law, to give his life as a ransom, to demonstrate God's love for us, and to make way for redemption and hope. During his earthly ministry, he took on our sin and shame. He was brought to trial and convicted unlawfully. As he was led away to be crucified, he was mocked and beaten and despised by the very people he came to save.

As Christians we share the story of Jesus's death, the greatest injustice to ever take place, knowing it is a story that also brings life and wholeness. We testify who Jesus is so that others may be liberated. It is a story that heals and restores. It is a story that unifies. When we proclaim the good news, we trust that people will be freed from the bondage of sin and its consequences. To share the account of Jesus's crucifixion and resurrection is to face a history that is brutally unfair. Yet, his story of injustice becomes our story of redemption.

As Christ followers, we understand the power of sharing the gospel in its entirety—in all the brutal and audacious truths. In the same way, we must find the courage to share the truth of our nation's history and surrender it to Christ in all its brokenness and beauty. In so doing, we can trust that the Lord will reveal himself to us in ways beyond our comprehension. When we allow our story to be redeemed by his, we find the freedom in our earthly relationships to experience the gift of a common memory united in genuine fellowship.

Let us share history. Let us share his story.

Share History, Share His Story

> You are witnesses of these things.
>
> Luke 24:48 ESV

Reflection Questions

1. Read Luke 24:48. What are the missional implications of this verse?
2. As Christ's followers, how are we to understand history and our role in stewarding it?
3. What are some practical ways we can redress legacies of racial harm and pursue relational wholeness?

6

Know Your Opponent

For we do not wrestle against flesh and blood, but against the rulers, against the authorities, against the cosmic powers over this present darkness, against the spiritual forces of evil in the heavenly places.

EPHESIANS 6:12 ESV

Learn from Boxing

I LOVE BOXING. IT is a thing of beauty. People are often surprised to hear that one of the communities I enjoyed most is the boxing gym I joined in Pomona, California, years ago. Each time I walked in, a few things were true. I experienced complete welcome and belonging. I found support and encouragement. In the gym, no one set limits; the default expectation was growth and development. There was mutual respect and camaraderie. While some members were competitive fighters, the majority were there because they wanted a great workout. There were few egos and even fewer rivalries. The boxing gym was a diverse community with individuals across the

Know Your Opponent

spectrum of age, race, and socioeconomic status. It was intergenerational, multicultural, and multilingual. In terms of kingdom representation, the gym accomplished what I've longed to see in the American church.

As for the training, our routines were a mix of cardiovascular exercises, core strengthening, and drills that included punching combinations, defensive techniques, legwork, heavy bag practice, and sparring. We built an arsenal of tools and were challenged to learn new skills and develop old skills with greater agility, speed, and accuracy. The training was rigorous, both physically and mentally, and I loved it. The gym was also the place where I learned some of the greatest leadership lessons—nuggets of wisdom I could incorporate into my daily decisions. Here are several of my favorites:

Advance and Engage

When I first started boxing, my natural inclination was to tense up and pull back. I wanted to avoid getting punched at all costs. That was my ultimate goal but not my coach's. As I flinched and stepped back, he reminded me to advance and engage. "You mean, you want me to move toward the threat? No thank you!" It took some time for me to trust his words or at least test them out. The more he repeated them, the more I was persuaded. *Advance and engage.* Those words echoed in between the spaces of my fear and slow-growing courage. Over time, rather than clenching my muscles and retreating, I eased into a posture of elbows down, fists up, chin tucked, shoulders turned toward my opponent ever so slightly, feet shoulder-width apart, hips parallel to the ground, and on my toes, steadily moving forward. With each step, I gained confidence in my ability to assess, pivot, and respond to my opponent's maneuvers. The fight was no longer intimidating. I had developed the reflexes to respond defensively and evade or minimize the impact of incoming punches. Offensively, I was able to create openings to land some punches of my own.

Over and over, *advance and engage.* It became my mantra. Not only in the ring but in my personal and professional life.

Experiencing interpersonal conflict? *Advance and engage.* Presented with a problem that does not have a clear solution? *Advance and engage.* Facing disappointment or shame? *Advance and engage.* Losing motivation? *Advance and engage.* Coming to grips with loss? Well, grieve... and then *advance and engage,* and maybe grieve some more. This posture of advancing and engaging also helped in my Christian life as I started to understand the nature of spiritual warfare and the unseen battles raging all around us. In the spiritual realm, I discovered that advancing and engaging often required that I surrender and pray. A lesson well learned (and still learning).

Know Where the Ropes Are

During weekly training, we would enter the ring for light sparring. The goal was not to overcome our opponent, but rather, to get comfortable in a fight setting. We would practice our punching combinations and move through the defensive rhythms of slip, bob, and weave, all while gaining an awareness of our placement in the ring. While it is often necessary to fight off the ropes, and it can even be advantageous for a fighter when used effectively, most often boxers try to stay off the ropes and gain control of the center. For boxers, sensing when they are nearing the ropes becomes crucial to being able to pivot well and regain both positional and psychological advantage.

For me, knowing where the ropes were had become a metaphor for understanding how to maneuver through life, work, and relationships. I became more attuned to my environment with an ability to anticipate problems and identify solutions. I developed the capacity to stand against the ropes, literally and figuratively, and from that vantage point, gain hope, direction, and vision. From the ropes, I also glimpsed how Satan can ensnare and entangle me in sin and doubt. Equipped with wrist guards and gloves, I was reminded to put on the armor of God so I could stand more firmly against the enemy's attacks.

KNOW YOUR OPPONENT

Use Resistance to Grow

I learned that having a good boxing partner is essential to growth. If you have ever done focus mitt drills, you know the difficulty when your partner does not provide the necessary resistance. Putting your force behind a punch, only to have the focus mitt flap around, exerts so much energy. But punching against resistance allows for greater force, speed, strength, and momentum. In many ways, building our faith is similar. To grow in our understanding of God's love toward us and our kingdom mandate to love others, we must face resistance. In our differences and conflict we discover the limits of our capacity to love and discover our need for the Holy Spirit—the only means by which we embrace others with a Godly love.

Develop Unshakable Footing

When I first started boxing, I could not understand why we focused on core and leg exercises. After all, isn't throwing a heavy punch about having upper body strength? As I trained more, I discovered what our coach had been telling us all along. Our power comes from our legs, so I spent a significant amount of time developing my stance and footwork. Distancing my feet appropriately. Remaining perched on my toes with my knees slightly bent, allowing for that boxer's bounce. I spent a lot of time jumping rope and varying my patterns and pace—slow, fast, uneven, crisscross, double under, hopping, skipping, shuffling. It all served to challenge and develop my footwork, to hone my timing, coordination, and agility, and to increase my cardiovascular capacity. The lesson in boxing training, like so much of life, was the importance of developing unshakable footing.

To withstand an opponent, we must know the ground upon which we are standing. We must be prepared for maneuvers that might set us off balance. And, when (not if) we stumble, we must have enough dexterity to regain our footing. This applies to the Christian life. We can become blinded to the enemy's tactics, and unless we are tethered to God's word, we are likely to find ourselves sucker punched and knocked out before the final round.

Know Your True Opponent

In a boxing match, you know your opponent. The individual may be someone you have fought before or someone entirely new. Either way, you know their name, their stats, and their fighting strengths and weaknesses. Before a match, you watch footage of their earlier matches to better understand how they fight and how you should prepare. In boxing, your opponent is the person standing in front of you who has agreed to the fight and is matched to your weight class.

Outside of boxing, knowing our opponent is often less clear. It is all too easy to name the individual with whom we have deep disagreement as the enemy. Satan loves division and wants us to believe that our true battle is with the person in front of us. Yes, there are true flesh and blood opponents, but we must also remain wide awake and recognize when Satan is diverting our attention, causing us to tear at one another, separating us from God, and dimming our witness.

Learn from Biblical Figures

Throughout Scripture we can find Satan's tactic of deceive and divide. From Gen 3, we learn that Satan is cunning. He twists God's words to sow doubt and uncertainty so that Eve questions what God has already made clear about eating from the tree of knowledge of good and evil. Eve's husband, Adam, follows suit and becomes a victim of the enemy's wiles. Almost immediately after the Bible's first couple becomes aware of their sinfulness, the blame game begins. Once confronted by God, Adam quickly accuses Eve.

There are few places in the Bible where we see Satan's nature and tactics more explicitly than in the book of Job. We learn that Satan is roaming the earth seeking to divide and harm. He is unabashed in his intent to destroy. He confronts the Lord and seeks to test his tactics on God's faithful follower, Job. The Lord grants permission with one caveat: Satan is not to harm Job physically (Job 1:12). Satan takes this challenge to the fullest extent and tests Job in an attempt to get him to curse God. Satan begins by stealing Job's livestock and killing his sheep, servants, and children. When Satan sees Job is unwavering in his faith, he destroys Job's house and health. Although Satan is ultimately unsuccessful in his efforts, we see the extent to which he will go to shatter faith and break ties to God.

Follow Scripture to the Gospel of Luke, and we see how Satan uses pride and arrogance to deceive and divide. In one of the most dramatic moments of Scripture, we approach the last moments of Jesus's life. As the disciples partake in one final meal with their teacher and friend, Jesus warns the disciples that one among them would betray him. In their pride, they bicker about who would do such a thing, and they argue about who among them is the greatest. Jesus predicts it will be Peter, but Peter is overly confident in his loyalty. Fast forward to the garden of Gethsemane. It is the night before Jesus's crucifixion. Jesus instructs his disciples to pray so they don't fall into temptation. Jesus then drops to his knees and cries out in agony to the Father, praying there would be another way for him to fulfill his mission as Savior. The disciples fall asleep instead, and Jesus once again instructs them to pray. In the next scene, Jesus is arrested, and Peter denies knowing him. Realizing he had given into Satan's temptation, Peter "wept bitterly" (Luke 22:62 ESV), heartbroken that he had forsaken the one he has followed and served.

On the night before his death, Jesus prays not only for his disciples but for all who will come to know him and the power of his death and resurrection. It is significant that in his final prayer before being arrested and taken to the cross, Jesus asks specifically for all believers to be brought into the unity of the Trinity. By extension, we can understand Jesus's desire for us to live in unity with one another as radical evidence to the world that there is a Great Redeemer. Of all the things Jesus could have prayed at the end of his earthly ministry, why did he pray for oneness? Because it is core to our mission and purpose. From creation, we were made in the likeness of God, designed to dwell in perfect fellowship with him. This plan was thwarted when Satan stirred discord and brought separation. But God promised to send a Savior who would restore us to right relationship. As Jesus draws near to the cross, he knows that promise is about to be fulfilled. While the emphasis in John 17:20–26 is on the kind of oneness we are to experience with God the Father, Son, and Holy Spirit, we are also empowered to live in union with one another and renounce the enemy's efforts to divide.

Hold Back the Darkness

If we understand the powers of darkness that Paul the apostle talked about when advising the church of Ephesus to take up the whole armor of God, we understand that our role in spiritual warfare includes both remembering the One who has already defeated every enemy and waging against the "forces of evil in the heavenly places" (Eph 6:12 ESV). I was reminded of this lesson a number of years ago when I participated in a Race, Trauma, and Gospel Experience in Montgomery, Alabama. The three-day event, hosted jointly by the Impact Movement (Atlanta, Georgia) and Allender Center (Seattle, Washington), brought together faith leaders from church and parachurch organizations, as well as Christian colleges and universities. This wasn't a typical conference; rather, it was the first of several events intended to engage pastors, academic leaders, and practitioners in the work of racial reconciliation.

The fact that the event was held in Montgomery, Alabama—a city shaped by slavery—was not inconsequential. During the three-day event, we visited the National Memorial for Peace and Justice, a site of remembrance dedicated to the history of lynching in the United States, and the Legacy Museum, which documents the history of racism in America from slavery to mass incarceration. Following these visits, we participated in mixed-race-facilitated discussion groups—an opportunity to reflect on and discuss what we observed and learned. The responses varied. After visiting the National Memorial, several leaders of color reported that they identified the names of family members who were victims of racial lynchings. White participants grappled with the weight of the history they encountered and their responsibility to remain historically informed. Collectively, we expressed our visceral response to the images of racial terror displayed through sculpture, art, and monuments.

As I listened to the conversations around the room, I grew soul-weary. It's not that the conversations were bad. They were actually quite thoughtful. But they were just that, conversations—more words, more sentiments. When I spoke up, a colleague could sense my deep frustration. He asked how I was doing, and I confessed that I was angry. I was tired of talking about the history of racism without being able to do more to overcome its residual strength. In a moment of profound wisdom and care, he turned to me, gently placed his hand on my shoulder, and asked, "My sister. What if, for all your efforts, you don't see the changes you are looking for? What if *all* you are doing is holding back the darkness? Can that be enough?" More than six years later, I am still grappling with my colleague's words. I had not previously thought about the work of racial reconciliation and healing as a cosmic struggle. I still don't know exactly what my colleague had in mind. While I understood his words, the fullness of their meaning continues to unfold.

As Christians we are called to be peacemakers, but we are also called to fight. We are spiritual boxers who wrestle "against the rulers, against the authorities, against the cosmic powers over this present darkness" (Eph 6:12 ESV). In the battle against the one who deceives, we must establish a much more endurable arsenal of tools than wrist wraps and boxing gloves. We must develop the spiritual wisdom, practices, and postures that ready us to prevail against Satan's tactics as he attempts to separate us from God and one another.

Minister Reconciliation to Others

When we look at the polarization among believers today, building relationships across personal divides can seem like a daunting and even futile endeavor. We might ask,

- Why would we ever seek to create bridges with those who claim Jesus as Savior but whose views seem to contradict our own?
- Isn't it better to just avoid those with whom we experience polarity?
- As disciples of Jesus, won't our spiritual lives suffer if we engage with image bearers whose earthly perspective is so different from our own?
- Are there particular disagreements that should become nonnegotiable and render impotent our relationships with our Christian brothers and sisters?
- Under what conditions does our Christian faith compel us to dissociate?

Scripture is instructive here. The Bible tells us that dissociation is sometimes necessary to shield the church:

> I appeal to you, brothers, to watch out for those who cause divisions and create obstacles contrary to the doctrine that you have been taught; avoid them. For such persons do not serve our Lord Christ, but their own appetites, and by smooth talk and flattery they deceive the hearts of the naive. (Rom 16:17–18 ESV)

Yet, Scripture is equally clear that we are to be ambassadors of reconciliation who see others as God sees them—through the lens of redemption and with hope for restoration:

> From now on, therefore, we regard no one according to the flesh. Even though we once regarded Christ according to the flesh, we regard him thus no longer. Therefore, if anyone is in Christ, he is a new creation. The old has passed away; behold, the new has come. All this is from

God, who through Christ reconciled us to himself and gave us the ministry of reconciliation; that is, in Christ God was reconciling the world to himself, not counting their trespasses against them, and entrusting to us the message of reconciliation. Therefore, we are ambassadors for Christ, God making his appeal through us. We implore you on behalf of Christ, be reconciled to God. For our sake he made him to be sin who knew no sin, so that in him we might become the righteousness of God. (2 Cor 5:16–21 ESV)

We can approach disagreements with the understanding of our new creation identity and the confidence that God is at work.

Follow the Narrative Arc

There are lessons, too, in the very design of the biblical narrative. In Bartholomew and Goheen's *The Drama of Scripture: Finding Our Place in the Biblical Story*, we read that the gospel story is crafted intentionally around a beautiful arc—creation, fall, and redemption. This is the story we have inherited. This is the story of which we are a part, and it follows a particular order. The opening scene is creation, a display of God's abundance and grace and an overflow of the love he had for his Son that could not be contained. So begins the gospel story.

This love is powerful enough to bridge the chasm between a holy God and a fallen people. When sin entered the world and separation became our fate, God had already orchestrated a way for his beloved to return to him. While separation is a necessary by-product of humankind's disobedience, we were never to be left in our state of alienation. God's intent has always been for us to be redeemed, restored, and made whole. Separation is the rival to God's divine plan, and we must, therefore, allow our relational patterns to conform to the arc of the biblical narrative—creation, fall, and redemption. Unity does not mean that every relationship will be healed this side of heaven. Some human relationships are too destructive for us to maintain. There are abuses so great that it would be unwise to remain in relational proximity. But our posture must, first and foremost, align with God's overarching plan to bring unity to all things in Christ:

> In him we have redemption through his blood, the forgiveness of our trespasses, according to the riches of his grace, which he lavished upon us, in all wisdom and insight making known to us the mystery of his will, according to his purpose, which he set forth in Christ as a plan for the fullness of time, to unite all things in Christ, things in heaven and things on earth. (Eph 1:7–10 ESV)

Through his death and resurrection, Christ has revealed his power over our true opponent while making a way for us to be restored to God and one to another.

For we do not wrestle against flesh and blood, but against the rulers, against the authorities, against the cosmic powers over this present darkness, against the spiritual forces of evil in the heavenly places.

EPHESIANS 6:12 ESV

Reflection Questions

1. Read Eph 6:12. What does this passage teach us about the root causes of our separation from God and each other?
2. Amid cultural division, how can we discern our true enemies and fight rightly?
3. What might the biblical story arc have to teach us about how we are to live out Christ's reconciling love in the face of conflict and strife?

7

Remember and Forget, Constructively

You shall remember that you were a slave in the land of Egypt, and the Lord your God redeemed you; therefore, I command you this today.

DEUTERONOMY 15:15 ESV

Remember not the former things, nor consider the things of old. Behold, I am doing a new thing; now it springs forth, do you not perceive it? I will make a way in the wilderness and rivers in the desert.

ISAIAH 43:18–19 ESV

Unexpected Lessons from an Unexpected Diagnosis

"YOU LOOK SO HANDSOME, Dad." The words barely pushed past the lump in my throat. There my dad stood in his Sunday best, ready for church. He looked really nice that day. Everything seemed to be in order, but I noticed he put on my mother's black overcoat.

Remember and Forget, Constructively

"Dad, put this one on instead, okay?" I didn't want to draw attention to the fact that he no longer recognized ordinary things. It was the last time my dad would visit me in California. I was glad to have him there, but I was also sad most of the visit. So much of Dad's memories had already faded. All we had left were flickers—moments of lucidity when it seemed things were normal. Those moments were followed by angry outbursts, or worse yet, a dulling vacancy that made evident the person we loved was no longer fully there.

As Dad's Alzheimer's progressed, he sensed something was wrong. I'm not sure he ever heard the word *Alzheimer's*. My father was adamant about not going to doctors, so it wasn't until he advanced to severe mental diminishment and could no longer protest that we had a diagnosis. Even without a formal diagnosis, we knew, and so did Dad. "Something's just not right," he would say. "My stomach doesn't feel right." Dad was not a man who expressed feelings, so for him to acknowledge *anything* was wrong was the only indicator I needed. Dad was not okay, and he was not going to be okay.

One of the most difficult parts was watching Alzheimer's take away his physical strength. Gradually, Dad lost weight. His muscles atrophied, and his height decreased. My father was never a tall man. He peaked at five feet nine, but now I could almost stand shoulder to shoulder. Yes, age was a factor, but the main culprit was the disease. Alzheimer's seemed unnecessarily cruel. "You're taking his mind, but his body, too? Does he have to lose *everything*?" Inevitably, Dad had to stop working. Alzheimer's made it so he could no longer drive. My father had always been a great driver, and he enjoyed it. But driving, like so many other daily activities, had become confusing and overwhelming. One day, my father relayed that someone had been honking at him. He couldn't understand why, but as he described what happened, we realized Dad had been sitting at the intersection far too long. He had lost the ability to understand the difference between a green light and a red light. We should have taken his keys sooner, but in our grief, there was also denial.

Homeward

The final blow was when Dad started wandering. He walked incessantly in his anxiety and confusion. While Mom continued to care for him, it became increasingly difficult to keep him safe. The day Dad went missing is when we knew something had to change. We finally decided to place him in a nursing home. There is a sad relief accompanied by a defeating resignation in admitting a loved one to long-term care.

But, in God's goodness, some remarkable things were happening too. As Dad's physical capacity decreased, his innermost being grew in strength. There were tender moments that had been locked behind the chaos in his mind. As heaven pierced years of suppressed trauma, we could see the person Dad might have been without the scars of childhood abandonment and abuse.

I remember visiting him in the nursing home and seeing his smile as he greeted me. Dad hadn't recognized anyone for some time, so God's grace in that moment seemed particularly sweet. He not only called me by name but also smiled with the most honest and endearing smile. It was the look I longed for most of my life.

While I was grateful for those glimpses into God's inner workings, I remained heartbroken by the reality of Alzheimer's. I cried often in those days. Sometimes the tears created a steady flow of seawater to my lips. Other times the tears fell gradually, hitting my cheeks with a pulsating drip that marked the passing of time. Occasionally, I cried but had no tears, leaving a tightness in my throat that felt like choking on sadness.

I believe Alzheimer's robbed my father of much, but I also believe it helped to blot out the pain of his past and reveal his true heart. When you are losing a loved one to a debilitating disease, it is difficult to say there is beauty in it. *But God.* As my father began to lose his grip on this world, a peace drew him into the presence of God. No more toiling seven days a week. No more fears. No more sadness. That little boy who lost his mother at age five and was placed in a children's home no longer had to search for home. When all is lost and nothing stands between here and eternity, the road to freedom is clear.

Remember and Forget, Constructively

Alzheimer's is a brutally cruel condition, and for anyone suffering from its fate, I would never want to diminish the impact. Alzheimer's isn't a choice, and losing your memory is fatally unfair. Yet, I believe it has something to teach us about the role of remembering and forgetting in the process of growing toward unity and relational wholeness.

Echoes and Silences: The Power of Memory and Forgetting

I've discovered in relationships that remembering and forgetting constructively can be essential to living faithfully amid division. *Remembering* allows us to acknowledge where we have been. I sometimes find it helpful to journey through history and to revisit, for instance, the laws and practices of Jim Crow, the residue of which lingers in our communities. By remembering, we can critically examine the conditions that have shaped and formed our current landscape, and we can continue to work toward a regenerative future. The practice of remembering allows us to honor where God has taken us individually and collectively and to acknowledge which experiences have both tested and strengthened our faith. It can curtail our natural tendency toward sinfulness. Remembering constructively also brings us into divine awareness of whose we are and how we are to conduct ourselves in holy communion with the Father and with one another.

Forgetting constructively can be an act of handing our brokenness over to Christ, the author and finisher of our faith that he might "bin[d] up [our] wounds" (Ps 147:3 ESV) and "fulfill his purposes for [us]" (Ps 138:8 ESV). In doing so, we open the door to forgiveness, making space for the Holy Spirit to intervene on our behalf in those areas where division, hatred, resentment, anger, fear, and revenge have taken residence. Forgetting constructively is not about becoming indifferent to wrongdoing; instead, it is about disremembering the pattern of violence that is created within us with each atrocity. At least, this is what I have discovered time and again as a fellow sojourner, navigating a polarized world marked by racial estrangement and marred by racial hatred.

As a Black woman, each time I see a news report of a Black male murdered in an act of racial violence, I experience a reinjury. The present image of violence connects with my knowledge of the previous, and the one before that. Ahmaud Arbery becomes Trayvon Martin. Trayvon Martin becomes James Byrd Jr. James Byrd Jr. becomes Emmett Till. While I am focused on the immediate incident, I am simultaneously swept into a repetitive narrative—a historical loop reminding me of the enduring nature of racism and the insidious ways it manifests in social life.

In each moment of reinjury a rage sears within me. My fight-or-flight reflex spurs me to react, but as a "good Christian," I have learned to live civilly, which simply means that I know my anger cannot erupt in public spaces and that even in private, I must temper my outrage. In those moments when racial wounds have been ripped open, the response from majority-culture peers is often an unimpassioned acknowledgment of the wrongdoing. Like a dull knife that requires more pressure to cut its object, the passive response from a neighbor, coworker, or friend can leave jagged edges around my heart. To prevent the buildup of too much scar tissue, I seek ways to immediately begin the mending process. I cannot wait for others to understand or empathize with what it means to live as the racialized other. My urgency is to disremember the pattern of injury that wells up in my body and seeks to cripple my soul.

To be clear, in this context forgetting is not the same as denial. It is not suppression. It is not about condoning or being complicit with past wrongs. It is not about discounting the depth of the offense, nor is it a display of resignation. To the contrary, forgetting is an act of great clarity and choice, as well as a spiritual move toward healing. It is an act of resistance against the kind of forgetting that I am often asked to do by those who are fortunate enough to be disassociated from racial despair.

Remembering and forgetting constructively, while remaining hopeful in the work of racial redemption, provides a way to grasp truth while standing with unclenched fists, arms extended, and palms opened. In this posture we can beseech the Holy Spirit to keep us in his grace. In this posture we can search for a return to the pattern of remembering and forgetting that recurs throughout the Christian narrative.

We can return to the words of Moses in Deut 8 as he urges the Israelites to remember God's leading and faithfulness in the wilderness and to obey the Lord's commandments so that they can maintain their covenant with God. We can hold fast to the words of the psalmist in Ps 77 who in his despair recalls God's deeds and, in doing so, teaches us how to live in a place of hope and remembrance. We can grasp the love of Jesus in Matt 26:26–29, which reminds us that his blood has washed away our sins and restored us to God in the New Covenant. Scripture is clear—we are to remember that God has redeemed us. Yet, we are also to forget those things that are old—our past sin, failure, and ways of being—and to keep our focus on Christ (Phil 3:12–14).

The Truth About Memory in Global Truth and Reconciliation Efforts

Throughout history, people have used these God-inspired practices of remembering and forgetting constructively to respond to some of the most unjust and inhumane systems designed to bring division. One such example is the work of global truth and reconciliation commissions. Under various names, nations across the globe have initiated truth commissions to investigate politically motivated human rights violations and to restore communities to wholeness (e.g., Bolivia's National Commission of Inquiry into Disappearances, Chad's Commission of Inquiry into Crimes and Misappropriations, and Chile's National Truth and Reconciliation Commission). Among the most widely recognized is South Africa's Truth and Reconciliation Commission (TRC), founded by Nelson Mandela in 1995 following the period of apartheid rule.

The South African TRC remains in the minds of many as one of the most successful efforts in documenting human rights violations and seeking healing for deep divisions across class, race, and communal lines. Yet, the commission's focus on the actions of individuals is now recognized as a major shortcoming of South Africa's truth and reconciliation efforts, with some arguing that absent from this process was an honest and systemic engagement with structural violence.[1] According to Terry Dowdall, clinical psychologist at the University of Cape Town, the TRC fell short in two other important ways.[2] First, the process of recounting gross violations of human rights and opening the wounds of apartheid resulted in both material and psychological consequences for victims and perpetrators alike. Second, the TRC failed to provide adequate financial reparation for victims of apartheid violence.

Central to the work of the TRC was the African concept of *ubuntu*, which translated from the Zulu phrase "Umuntu ngumuntu ngabantu" means "I am, because you are." The principle of ubuntu, with its focus on the interdependence of members of community, highlighted the important role of forgiveness in restoring a nation marked by separateness (i.e., *apartheid* is an African word that means separation or apartness). Yet ubuntu offers a means to justice not fulfilled by calls for retribution and vengeance. In fact, ubuntu theology recognizes that "there is no future without forgiveness."[3] Without forgiveness, humanity as conceived in community cannot thrive. Forgiveness is the active pursuit of community, calling us to address those very areas of woundedness that would create fractures, separation, isolation, and fear. It mediates between the perfect love of God and the atrocities of humankind and allows us to live beyond our fallen condition. It releases us from the bondage of sin, such that we see each other within the grand scheme of God's kingdom. Our common humanity "makes forgiveness a matter of grasping another's narrative precisely where it intersects one's own, namely, at the place of injury."[4] Furthermore, forgiveness necessitates that we "remembe[r] and embrac[e] hurt

---

1. Mamdani, "Amnesty or Impunity."
2. Dowdall, "Psychological Aspects."
3. Haws, "Suffering, Hope and Forgiveness," 485.
4. Haws, "Suffering, Hope and Forgiveness," 485.

as the reality of a broken world in order to overcome 'the power of the injury, healing it in a new bond of union between [offender and offended].'"[5]

But forgiveness is not unidimensional, and in communal contexts, forgiveness often requires an element of forgetting that is necessary for true restoration. Dr. Rosalind Shaw, associate professor emerita at Tufts University, conducted field research in Sierra Leone for decades. She noticed that similar to South Africa's TRC, Sierra Leone's truth and reconciliation hearings emphasized a public recounting of memories of violence. However, Shaw also recognized that different regions of the world hold different beliefs about memory's role in bringing restoration. In places like Sierra Leone where civil war raged for more than a decade, local forms of recovery and reintegration also included social forgetting—that is, "the refusal to reproduce the violence by talking about it publicly."[6]

Perhaps we might learn from these historical moments. Is it possible that a global emphasis on remembering in truth and reconciliation commissions as well as local practices of social forgetting can serve as complementary models for those who are committed to walking toward unity? I believe they can. Both provide spiritual tools for personal and collective healing where human divisions have harmed God's beloved community.

Surely, human rights violations oppose God's plan, and it would be impossible in our carnal capacity to find unity where such crimes have occurred. Yet, restoration is still God's desire. In Isa 43:19, God declared that he was doing a new thing. In the death and resurrection of Jesus, he was bringing light to darkness, breaking down strongholds and division, and overcoming the power of sin and death. This does not mean that sin no longer manifests in the world. Nor does it mean that all dividing lines will be removed from our social fabric. As we dwell on earth, we will see economic and political strife, and cultural rifts will tear individuals and communities apart. The reality of disunity should not leave us complacent or hopeless. Instead, it should spur us toward sanctification

5. Haws, "Suffering, Hope and Forgiveness," 485.
6. Shaw, *Rethinking Truth and Reconciliation*, 9.

as an ongoing process of bringing healing to those places in our heart and relationships that have been fractured by our original separation from God.

We know that disunity opposes God's desire for restoration. Unity, on the other hand, can be understood as wholeness or completeness. It is a return to the state of communion that our first parents had in God's presence—a condition of the heart unimpaired by rebellion and strife. What then is our responsibility in the work of unity? We must *remember* the Lord's everlasting covenant (Ezek 37:11–28), with an understanding that the work of restoration is forever sealed with the blood of Christ. Empowered by the Holy Spirit, we must *forget* our old ways of being and incline our hearts toward Christ. Where disunity exists in our lives, we must grasp every opportunity to seek resonance with one another, which is different from agreement. The ultimate goal is not sameness but wholeness—a wholeness that reflects God's own character.

The Promise of Restoration

If our purpose on earth is to love God and to show that same love to others so that they may know him, our most vocal claims must first point to Christ's identity and mission in the world. If we truly understand what it means to be in the presence of Almighty God, we will turn from our disagreements more readily and run toward unity with a God-honoring urgency that will rattle the earth and draw our eyes to his breathtaking wonder. The purpose of our lives in unity is to reflect a glorious God, worthy of our praise. It should be our greatest desire that God will be exalted—that his love will be known not by what we say we believe, but by what we demonstrate in our willingness to move toward one another in the promise of restoration of all things.

If we understand the power of unity in Christ and are committed to seeking restoration and relational wholeness, we can allow our differences to draw us closer together. Those differences should open a gracious space to engage with a discerning curiosity that will spur us to more questions—authentic questions that reflect the humility and invitation extended by Christ's sacrifice on the cross. With clear perception, we can engage across differences with an expansiveness of heart that testifies to God's triumph over Satan and the division Satan sought to condemn us to.

The journey to unity begins with a willingness to step into each other's stories, understanding that our interconnectedness is wrapped in God's grand story and sealed in God's victory. Entering the spaces that separate us requires that we pause long enough to hear unexpected responses that might transform us and help us see God more clearly. It necessitates that we remain diligent in listening well, seeking understanding, and trusting that the Holy Spirit is present and active and leading us into deeper community and truth. In so doing, we can step into our inheritance of unbroken wholeness. As the late Tim Keller reminded us, "When we understand the mercy of God, it will always take us in the direction we would rather not go, toward people we would rather not care about, and ultimately into the deepest counsels of God."[7]

It is in the deepest counsels of God that we encounter his perfect will for us as bearers of his name. It is here that we see God's desire to restore us into right relationship and personal fellowship with himself through his Son Jesus Christ. It is here that we can experience the gift of memory as we recall his promises. It is here that we experience the grace of forgetting as we understand that God has forgiven our sins and remembers them no more.

---

7. Keller, "Jonah and the Mystery."

You shall remember that you were a slave in the land of Egypt, and the Lord your God redeemed you; therefore, I command you this today.

> DEUTERONOMY 15:15 ESV

Remember not the former things, nor consider the things of old. Behold, I am doing a new thing; now it springs forth, do you not perceive it? I will make a way in the wilderness and rivers in the desert.

> ISAIAH 43:18–19 ESV

Reflection Questions

1. What is the context of Deut 15:15 and Isa 43:18–19? What is the significance of these passages for us today?
2. What does it mean to forget in the context of forgiveness and healing?
3. What does it mean to remember in the context of forgiveness and healing?

Conclusion
A Prayer for the Journey Home

> And we all, with unveiled face, beholding the glory of the Lord, are being transformed into the same image from one degree of glory to another. For this comes from the Lord who is the Spirit.
>
> 2 CORINTHIANS 3:18 ESV

Emulating a Mother's Love

I HAVE THE KIND of mother who packed school lunches every day, ironed and darned clothes, and stood in as pitcher on days when my siblings and I wanted to play a pickup game of kickball. She was our cheerer at school events, audience member for our make-believe stage performances, and all-around homework checker, quizzer, and tutor. She methodically sectioned and braided my sister's and my hair on Saturday mornings, the official designated hair-wash day. She was the bookkeeper for my father's electrical subcontracting business and chief operations officer for our household.

My mom has always been physically attractive and admired for her curly hair and flawless skin. She's never worn makeup or adorned herself with exquisite jewelry or clothing. Her style is understated, yet she radiates a noticeable beauty. She ages with a grace that instructs. As I mature, I hope to set aside my vanity long enough to learn and master the same skill.

Homeward

My mom has lived a quiet and selfless life—never seeking attention for herself or making her desires paramount. To this day, she moves through the world with a cautious hesitation and measured sense of wonder. My siblings and I could never convince her to ride a bike or drive a car. She prefers the assurance of solid ground beneath her feet and has walked more miles and traveled more bus routes than anyone I know. Even though she's seventy-eight, daily walks remain a steady part of her diet. Grace is her signature trait, and her steps leave a footprint far more pronounced than her five-foot frame should produce. With every step she leaves a legacy of kindness and wisdom for others to follow.

She is an avid reader who discovers the full range of life experiences—friendship, adventure, tragedy, mystery, romance—between the pages of a book. It is not uncommon for my mom to visit the local library several times a week. She is the only one I know who can leave the library disappointed because there are no new books for her to read. She encounters characters from all walks of life. In this sense she is the most prolific traveler and cultural guide I know.

She is patient beyond measure. Throughout my childhood, it seemed she spent countless hours in the kitchen preparing traditional Jamaican dishes and doing so without many modern conveniences. I remember watching my mother grate coconut and squeeze the coconut milk to prepare rice and pigeon peas (gungu beans). When she baked, Mom would cream the butter by hand. With the bowl under her left arm and wooden spoon in her right hand, she would repeatedly blend and smooth the mixture. For fresh-squeezed carrot juice all she used was a box grater and fine mesh strainer. As a child, I would watch her at the stove to see when a johnnycake or plantain would come out of the frying pan so I could sneak a piece. I was never patient enough for it to cool. Rather than grow frustrated, my mom would simply set a piece aside and remind me to blow on it.

Mom created rhythms for ordinary tasks and brought order and calm to our house. Peace followed her wherever she went, and so did I. Whether she was crocheting doilies, sewing patches on

CONCLUSION

torn jeans, hanging laundry on the clothesline, or handwashing soiled socks on a scrub board, there was a pattern and purpose in everything, and you couldn't help but watch and get swept into her cadence.

As I've observed my mother over the years, I've acquired many lessons.

Live simply.
Show and earn respect.
Dress modestly.
Be kind to others.
Do your best—that's all you can do.
Keep your house clean.
Seek happiness and wish the same for others.
Good penmanship matters; so does proper grammar.
Be humble.
Don't air your dirty laundry or gossip.
Work hard and live a good life.

Nothing too complicated, just simple commonsense lessons.

It wasn't until I became an adult that I started to see my mom more fully and complexly—as a woman, a daughter, a wife, a child of God. As my father's Alzheimer's progressed, my previous notions of what constitutes strength were replaced by the image of my mom's steadfast and composed love. Taking on the very physical demands of his care was one thing, but what stood out more was her unshakable peace. At one point, I asked how she could remain so calm and assured as his behavior became more unpredictable and aggressive. She simply replied, "I am not afraid." I think it's the first time I knew my mom was not only a great mother and wife but an amazing warrior whose strength and quiet leadership came from a source I was only beginning to understand.

I continue to learn more about my mom with each passing year. Like the fact that she would have loved to have played the drums when she was younger. That is the last instrument I would have guessed for someone so reserved. I imagine we are all a bundle of paradoxes, mysteries, and possibilities. Recently, I learned that Mom loves romance novels and is a true romantic at heart who sometimes feels a bit of sadness when she sees older couples taking a walk, holding hands, and showing affection—something she wished for in her life.

Two summers ago, my mother visited Jon and me in our new home in East Texas. When we first moved to Gilmer, I remember sharing with my mom that it reminded me of her childhood home in Treasure Beach—the humidity, the beautiful sunrises above the open pastures, the way the trees canopied over the country roads. All we lacked was the beach. I couldn't quite understand how God shaped this full-circle life—that as the child of Jamaican immigrants I would find my way back to a place so reminiscent. I was so grateful and excited to share the experience with her.

Little did I know Mom would arrive for her visit the day after East Texas experienced its worst storm in nearly twenty years. To make matters worse, temperatures were reaching triple digits and power outages halted most normal activities. When I picked my mom up from the airport, I immediately apologized and explained that her visit wouldn't be very good since most of our plans would need to be canceled.

Mom wasn't concerned or disappointed. She had long discovered the gift of finding contentment in the simple pleasures of life. We spent that weekend going on early morning walks; sitting outside in the evenings and enjoying the views and sounds over the pasture; going to church; talking, sharing, reading, and laughing; attending the annual hot-air balloon festival; eating at my favorite local Mexican restaurant; and visiting with neighbors.

At the end of my mom's trip, Jon and I revisited pictures from our time together. One continues to capture my attention. Jon had taken a picture of me and my mom on a walk. I couldn't help but laugh as I noticed the similarities. Our short, curly hair and glasses. The color and style of our clothing. The way we swung our arms and planted our feet. The length of our stride. Our posture and frame. I don't know when it happened, but at some point, I became my mom. It didn't occur in a singular moment but over a long arc of time and space, sneaking up on me without my permission but welcomed all the same.

CONCLUSION

Reflecting the Father's Heart

Becoming like my mom is the cumulative result of years of observing and mimicking her patterns, receiving and giving the love she shares, and absorbing her wisdom and practicing it. Through steady and constant relationship with my mom, I've collected an abundance of treasures and gifts safely gathered in the storehouse of my heart. These resources guide and strengthen me through daily valleys and mountains and become a compass for living.

There are important parallels between the process of becoming more like my mom and my ongoing pursuit of God's heart. Both begin with relationship. Both require dedicated time and meaningful engagement. They are nurtured in the face of tests and trials. And they demand trust and intimacy. It is true that we emulate those we draw close to, which is good news when it comes to following our Maker and Redeemer.

The Christian life is about becoming more like Jesus in every aspect of our lives and proclaiming our true home in God. This book has been about our journey home. More precisely, it has been about the process of returning to a state of unbroken wholeness and conforming to Christ in our relationships through the power of the Holy Spirit. The chapters have offered personal reflections and insights in the form of seven redemptive moves—small but purposeful acts that might bring meaningful change as we seek to imitate Christ in how we love and interact with one another across racial and cultural divides as part of the essential work of Christian formation.

As we briefly revisit the seven redemptive moves, I hope you will identify one or two that you'd like to grow in. Then, commit to praying about how you might incorporate these postures in your life. The appendix that follows offers practical strategies for implementation, but please resist the temptation to skip to the back of the book in search of an answer key. Be patient. Rest in his love. Allow God to reveal deeper truths about what it might mean to respond to the call to greater understanding, healing, and wholeness across the divides.

Keep the Second Half

God met our greatest need of all and changed the trajectory of our lives. His great love and compassion for us altered everything. Once we know this personal God who sent his Son to reach down into our broken places, it becomes a privilege to extend that reach to each other, joined in one fellowship (Gal 3:28), where we discover that each stranger is our neighbor. This is the principle at the heart of God's two-fold commandment to his people in Luke 10:27 ESV: "You shall love the Lord your God . . . *and your neighbor as yourself*" (italics added). Keeping the second half reminds us that we cannot experience genuine fellowship with Christ without simultaneously loving those we encounter. This commandment makes no exception based on race, national origin, political party, or any other basis of categorization. The kind of love that calls us to love our neighbors is all-encompassing and committed to achieving wholeness and shalom.

Embrace Disruptive Tensions

Jesus came to interrupt the world, to share a different way of living, and to set things right. He overturned tables in the temple because he saw it being misused. He disrupted social customs and norms when he approached the Samaritan woman at the well. He disrupted the Law and religious traditions associated with the ancient Israelites. With the coming of the Lamb, priests were no longer needed to enter the Holy Place. Instead, Jesus's death and resurrection made a way for believers to be restored to righteousness and for our bodies to become temples for God's spirit to indwell. Jesus's sacrifice on the cross also brought an end to all hostilities between God and his people. Jesus wants to disrupt the way we order our lives and relationships so we are no longer at enmity with one another. Yet, there is no easy way for us to get there. It cost Jesus everything on the cross, and it will cost us everything, too. Disruptive tensions are not to be avoided. They are to be embraced as part of our journey to the cross.

Conclusion

Test the Strength of Your Rope

Christians often profess their love of all people, but if this were true, we would not see so much division among God's people. As Howard Thurman reminds us, love is not theoretical. We do not come to love each other by way of our goodness. It is by the Spirit that we gain a revelation of God's love—a love that is incomprehensible but not beyond our reach (Eph 3:18–19). That revelation should transform our relationships—not only in terms of how we engage with each other but also with whom we seek proximity. Because segregation has been a normal part of our social landscape, many of us remain unaware of the distorted images and skewed perceptions limiting our capacity to truly see one another. In our homogeneous living, there is little opportunity to "test the strength of our rope"—to truly know what we believe about each other—and to maintain the deep fellowship required to reverse long-standing assumptions and hostilities. To fully experience the gift of unity and wholeness, we must allow encounters across difference to test our humanly love that our hearts may be refined by the fatherly love of God.

Be a Salve

We are ministers of reconciliation called to bring healing to a broken world. We know the One who has entered our story of pain and suffering, the great healer and comforter who restores (2 Cor 1:3). Because we know the One, we must see the ones in front of us with a perceptibility that compels us to listen with an intent to heal. That is what it means to be a salve. Practicing presence and entering the suffering of another was central to Jesus's ministry on earth and is a vital part of the Christian life. As Christians committed to unity and wholeness, we must learn to sit with others, to hear their story, and to remain curious through parts of the narrative that seem messy or unfamiliar when held against the standard of our own lives. We must commit to praying for understanding and revelation knowing that each person's story is uniquely formed and that it has a place in the larger narrative of God's people. This work begins with repentant hearts that yield to God's grace.

Share History, Share His Story

We are all witnesses to history, bearers of the human story, with a capacity to connect past to present and shape a future that can be redeemed by the grace of God. The stories we tell about ourselves, our nation, and why things are the way they are has huge implications for how we live together in covenant community. We cannot recover wholeness and right relationship with the telling of partial stories. The power of testimony, like the telling of history, is that God speaks through our stories. If God is in everything, then history is not simply a recounting of events, it is a retelling of a divine story. Any omission or distortion risks minimizing God's role in the story of humankind and his plan for redemption. As we seek to live together in our differences, we can discover the power of history and his story to defeat the enemy and transform lives.

Know Your Opponent

Although we are conditioned to believe that political adversaries and cultural strangers are our enemies, we have but one true opponent, a liar and deceiver who rejoices in our hopelessness (John 10:10) and delights in stirring up division and strife (Gal 5:15). Thankfully, we have authority over Satan through Christ Jesus. Through the indwelling of the Holy Spirit, full provision has been given for us to win the battle over our opponent. Yet, we grieve the Holy Spirit when we seek victory without setting right our relationships with one another. The Word instructs us to "Make every effort to live in peace with everyone and to be holy" (Heb 12:14 ESV). What does this mean? Is it possible to make peace with everyone? Whether or not we achieve unity is a matter that may be beyond our reach on this side of the new heaven and new earth. But we must live as though we can. To do anything else is to allow the enemy to hold us prisoners when God has already set us free from the bondage of division.

CONCLUSION

Remember and Forget, Constructively

We have a responsibility to remember. We also have a responsibility to forget. We can't breathe a Christ-giving love into our relationships without first understanding the original source of that love and our alienation from it. Remembering our own fallenness and the magnitude of Jesus's suffering on the cross necessitates that we put away old things. With new life in Christ, we are to "let all bitterness and wrath and anger and clamor and slander be put away from [us], along with all malice" (Eph 4:31 ESV). Remembering the "costly grace" that saved us requires that we also freely let go.[1] Unity requires that we never stray too far from our memory of the cross and the empty tomb or hold too tightly to the things that endeavor to divide.

Traveling Together

My own journey toward racial understanding and meaningful reconciliation and repair has been challenging over the years. Yet, it is the place where God has breathed life into my relationships, faith, and work. I wrote this book as an invitation for us to commit to an incomprehensible love that has the power to extend across all dividing lines. As disciples of King Jesus, we have more in common than not—a Father who loves us, a Savior who died and rose for us, and a common inheritance as joint heirs with Christ. While alienation has been our common fate, we can be sure that Jesus is our common hope and offers a way for us to return to God, our home.

As we travel together, this is my prayer for you:

May you know the gift of God's grace
That it might be magnified in your heart
And stretch outward and onward.

---

1. Bonhoeffer, *Cost of Discipleship*.

Homeward

May you look into the face of each stranger
As a reflection of God's splendor and majesty
And let every passing gaze unveil the mysteries of his love.

May your heart break open
to reveal the kingdom coming
And beat toward unity and wholeness.

May your tongue profess Christ's name
With a language and longing for his return
And be used to bring peace.

May you silence the chains of deception
That clang toward division and despair
And sing a new song of freedom.

May you find divine courage and strength
Knowing the battle ahead is long
And requires more than you have.

May you welcome the challenge
Finding in it, the life-breathing joy
And gift of the Holy Spirit to sustain.

May the cross be your teacher and guide
That you might grow in wisdom and truth
And be the salve that brings a healing sight.

May the empty tomb be your hope
Pointing you to the God of redemption
And restore you to his glory.

Amen.

CONCLUSION

And we all, with unveiled face, beholding the glory of the Lord, are being transformed into the same image from one degree of glory to another. For this comes from the Lord who is the Spirit.

2 CORINTHIANS 3:18 ESV

Reflection Questions

1. Read 2 Cor 3:18. What insights can you gain for participating in Christ's reconciling mission?
2. As you consider the seven redemptive moves introduced throughout this book, which do you find most challenging? Which resonate the most and offer encouragement in your pursuit of racial understanding and healing?
3. As you reflect on your own journey toward unity and wholeness, how might you invite others to join this work?

Appendix
A Practical Guide

THIS APPENDIX PROVIDES ACTIONABLE steps for each of the redemptive moves introduced in chapters 1 through 7. They are offered as suggestions rather than absolutes. I hope they serve as a helpful tool if you are looking for a starting point. Approach them, just as you have each chapter, as an invitation to live together in a world of difference with a love that sustains.

Chapter 1: Keep the Second Half

Pray for Spiritual Sight

Because our human eyes are spiritually myopic, we need help to see each other in God's image. That help comes from the Holy Spirit, and so, we must pray. We live in a context where social action sometimes takes precedence over inward spiritual disciplines. But prayer is the most powerful and productive activity we can engage in if we truly want to learn to love our neighbor. Here are some specific ways we can pray:

- for God to redeem our hearts and restore our vision to how he sees each of us as part of his good creation (Gen 1)
- against the lies and distortions we have accepted about various people groups

Appendix

- for discernment as we consume information outlets that play a significant role in deepening existing divides
- for the ability to redefine "neighbor" according to Scripture, in a way that goes beyond geographical proximity and cultural familiarity

Consider developing a prayer rhythm that deepens your understanding and capacity to engage across differences.

Look for God's Fingerprints

Have you ever taken the time to look at your fingerprint with its various ridge patterns? Yours is like no other person's. Your fingerprints are distinct and cannot be replicated. They were formed during your earliest development in the womb and remain the same throughout your lifetime. They are an enduring symbol of your originality and divine design. In their singularity, fingerprints are a reminder that everything in creation bears God's craftsmanship. This should cause us to respond to each individual with eyes of love. For, if we love God, we will love his creation, regardless of the things that divide. We will see each individual as bearing a unique mark given by the author. As we behold God's goodness, we won't dare to blemish those traces of his touch. Instead, we will do everything to preserve each element of God's handiwork.

So, as you sit across the dividing line, identify at least one or two attributes in each person that bear God's fingerprints. Meditate on God's intent for humankind. Place each individual in that divine plan, and simply accept the fact that they, too, are created and loved by God.

Renounce Racial Stereotypes

As we pray, we must also act. We must choose to consume information with an understanding of our responsibility to honor the God-given dignity in each person. We must consider how we are being shaped spiritually by the words, images, and ideas that circulate in common discourse. We must recognize how our perception of others is gradually perverted and disfigured by racial stereotypes.

While stereotypes may seem harmless and even humorous, if we consider them in light of a perfect God and his creation, we might take greater care and stewardship of what we allow our minds to conceive, mouths to utter, and ears to hear. We might find ourselves growing intolerant of anything that denigrates the image of God in others. We might grasp that making a "joke" at a national presidential rally about a Black attendee having been at a Halloween party carving watermelons is not simply distasteful, but evil when understood in the post-slavery context in which that stereotype was birthed.[1]

While we have a right to free speech that allows such depictions, as disciples of Christ we are called to holiness, and we must refuse to live beneath our calling. Whatever remains in our collective hearts that finds delight in denigrating others must be wrenched out. A love-driven ethic demands that we no longer allow God's image in others to be defaced.

Chapter 2: Embrace Disruptive Tensions

Stay in Difficult Conversations

When you find yourself in a conversation where you and the other individual are poles apart, challenge yourself to listen before speaking. When you choose to speak, be curious and ask questions that invite genuine dialogue rather than debate. Consider the following sentence starters:

- "I've not thought about it like that..."
- "That hasn't been my experience, but I'd like to hear more."

---

1. Here I refer to Tony Hinchcliffe's remarks at Republican presidential nominee and now President Donald Trump's campaign rally at Madison Square Garden in New York City on October 27, 2024.

Appendix

- "Would you be willing to share how you came to understand it that way?"

When you offer your perspective, be humble, sharing how your thinking came to be and using personal stories to illustrate, where possible. You might offer insights about where you are still formulating your position and pursuing more information to clarify and refine your thinking.

Conversations are sustained and healthy relationships grow where there is an opportunity for mutual exploration and discovery. While it may be uncomfortable, we can gain much by persisting through the tension respectfully. Ask yourself,

- In the past year has my relationship deepened with someone who voted differently from me in the most recent presidential election?

- Do my existing networks provide opportunity for engagement across divergent views? What would it take for that to occur? What would I have to give up? Is it worth it for the sake of unity? What might I gain?

Seek Righteousness over Rightness

When in difficult conversations, we can be tempted to solidify our position and prove our rightness to the opposing side. Yet, the mark of a disciple is one who pursues Christ and his righteousness. One way we can determine if we are aligning with God's will as we engage across differences is to look for evidence of fruits of the spirit. We can allow Gal 5:22–23 to be our guide.

As you navigate polarizing topics and conversations, consider the following:

- How are my words and actions a display of *love, joy, peace, patience, kindness, goodness, faithfulness, gentleness, self-control*?

- Which characteristics of the Holy Spirit are most difficult for me to live out when I am engaged in conversations with polarized views? Name those characteristics and commit to cultivating them.

Close Racial Distance

Seek opportunities to bridge the physical divide. We may never become a fully integrated society with neighborhoods and communities that reflect the diversity of God's kingdom. Even if that were possible, I'm not sure we could close the psychological distance that remains from the lingering effects of legally enforced segregation. Yet, we can try.

As individuals we can be intentional about closing the racial distance when choosing a place to live. We can seek greater racial balance in our workplaces each time we make a hiring decision—not to fill quotas, but with an awareness of where our hiring practices reflexively reinforce racial exclusions and hierarchies. When considering where to take our business and invest our dollars, we can make choices that disrupt the economic disparities undergirding social distance.

On a smaller scale, when we attend an event, we can choose to sit at a table with individuals who do not share our racial identity. We can visit a church that worships in a different style and cultural tradition from our own. When going to the movie theater, we can support a film that portrays the lives of those who don't share our background.

Chapter 3: Test the Strength of Your Rope

Be Honest with Yourself

Are there particular people groups that you struggle to love? Without shame or self-blame, identify the group or groups that come to mind.

- What is the first association you make when you think about the particular group(s) you named?

Appendix

- Are there stereotypes you've attributed?

Now, make it more personal.

- Is there a particular individual who comes to mind when you think about the group or groups you identified? Describe that person.
- What would you identify as their positive and negative attributes?
- Do you recall a specific interaction with that person that was difficult or uncomfortable?
- Or is your knowledge of the individual more distant and nonspecific (as in a public figure with whom you have no direct interaction)?
- Are you drawing conclusions based on evidence, or have your thoughts been formed within a generalized set of assumptions?

Take Stock of Your Networks

Take a sheet of paper and create a simple table with rows and columns. In the left-hand column, list the individuals you interact with routinely. This might include your spouse, closest friends, neighbors, your supervisor and coworkers, pastor, your child's teacher, your medical providers (primary physician, eye doctor, dentist). You may think of others. Within each cell of the top row, list various identity factors, including race, ethnicity, political affiliation, socioeconomic level, and religious affiliation. To the best of your ability, identify with a check mark the individuals who share your identity characteristics. Ask yourself the following questions:

- How diverse or homogeneous is my network?
- Do the individuals I interact with most frequently share my identity?

- Where diversity exists, to what extent does it occur within relationships of unequal status (e.g., supervisor to employee) that either reinforce or disrupt long-standing racial hierarchies?

For instance, it is rare for a White person to have a Black doctor or supervisor, but such a dynamic might challenge prevailing assumptions and allow for new insights and growth. Consider how you have been shaped and formed by social patterns that have become normative.

Assess Who Is Seated on the Throne

Fear and pride are two of the greatest obstacles to achieving relational wholeness and unity. In matters where racial and cultural tensions persist, fear and pride can manifest in the avoidance of contentious topics. Barriers of fear and pride also show up as learned helplessness, a posture of inability to adopt new patterns of behavior and thought that would contribute to healing across racial tensions. At times fear and pride appear as a selfish desire to maintain the world as it is, with racial hierarchies intact and dominant cultural norms and ideologies preserved without any disruption or change. Fear and pride can also manifest in an overindulgence in our cultural and political affiliations or our professional and social status, all to the detriment of our identity and formation in Christ.

We can be sure that any time our motivations are primarily driven by self-interest or self-preservation, we risk unseating Christ. To assess who is seated on the throne ask:

- When I encounter racial or cultural tensions, what do I turn to instead of God?
- Are there spiritual strongholds or idols of fear, anger, resentment, pride, or hostility that need to be rooted out?

- Is there anything in my life I would choose above God's commandments, including his commandment to love my neighbor?

Commit to ensuring that nothing takes God's place on the throne of your life.

Chapter 4: Be a Salve

Scan the Room

Notice who is represented in various contexts throughout your week. Actually count who is in the room in terms of racial representation and ask:

- To what extent are the rooms you occupy representative of God's kingdom?
- What do you observe about yourself in relation to those who are represented? Are you among the majority or minority? Is this typical of your experience?
- If you are never the minority in the room, pause for a moment and ask yourself why. The answer might seem obvious, but go a bit deeper. Is your representation in the room proportionate to population demographics in your community or profession, or is your majority status positively skewed?
- Consider who is underrepresented or not represented at all. What is your working hypothesis for explaining their absence? Are there any other possible explanations? Have you ever missed—that is, longed for—their presence in the room? If not, why?

Take some time to consider how you might be affected—relationally, spiritually, culturally—by their absence especially as you think about God's intent for diversity and his desire that we love *all* our neighbors. This activity may feel uncomfortable. That's okay, especially if it is the first time you are making observations about your cultural location.

A PRACTICAL GUIDE

Become a Radical Story Listener

Get to know the stories of those who do not share your background or perspective. Become relentlessly curious and seek opportunities to learn about the experiences of those whose lives are vastly different from your own. If your network is homogeneous, I am not suggesting that you approach strangers. If you don't have authentic ways to engage with individuals who do not share your racial or ethnic identity, start by reading memoirs, autobiographies, or works of historical fiction. Begin with literature written by members of the groups you identified earlier as being particularly difficult for you to love. Consider the context in which their lives emerged and developed. What unique challenges did they face? Where do you see particular moments of strength and resiliency?

As you have opportunity to do so, ask the individuals in your life to share their stories. There is no single starting point, but consider your setting and relationship with the person and adapt your questions accordingly. Be genuine and respectful. Only ask to hear their story if you are legitimately interested and able to be fully present. While being asked to share your story can be honoring, it can also be burdensome if you've had to explain your "differences" over a lifetime. So ask questions thoughtfully, insightfully, and sparingly, leaving enough room for the storyteller to feel comfortable to share and for future conversations to take place.

As you listen, suspend judgment. Resist the temptation to make an immediate moral assessment. Ask sincere questions that allow for genuine inquiry. Identify threads of commonality in the human experience. Cultivate understanding and compassion by identifying moments in their story where you relate to experiences of love, life, and loss.

Don't Minimize

One challenge I've experienced in race conversations is the "explaining away" or minimizing of lived experiences. If I share that my brother was recently questioned by three police officers while grocery shopping, I can expect a well-meaning friend to explain that the police were probably just responding to a call. Nothing racialized, just doing their job. I've often wondered what would be lost if the listener simply listened.

As you engage across differences, consider your own posture:

- In conversations about race, what is your first impulse when you hear someone describe a personal experience of racial discrimination or targeting?
- Are you inclined to believe their experience, or do you immediately seek justifications for what the person *assumed* to be racially motivated?
- Are you inclined to believe their experience but not the severity?
- Do you question what they might have been doing to provoke the response they received?
- What stands in your way of receiving another person's story as it is?
- What might you have to give up to receive their story? What might you gain?

As you gain awareness of your response, you can enter race conversations with greater cultural humility.

Chapter 5: Share History, Share His Story

Participate in God's Reconciling Work

Begin by studying Scripture to grasp the central reconciling mission of Jesus's testimony. Jesus's life and teachings centered on reconciling people with God and with one another. His death on the cross was an ultimate act of reconciliation. This is the work to which we have been invited. Take time to meditate on these key Scripture passages as a starting point for understanding your role in the ministry of reconciliation:

A PRACTICAL GUIDE

- 2 Corinthians 5:18–19
- Ephesians 2:14–16
- Galatians 3:28

What do these passages reveal about the nature of God and his redemptive plan? Write down your observations and reflections. Choose to participate in the work. Make one small commitment (e.g., for the next month, I will commit to twenty minutes each day to studying Scripture and expanding my knowledge of God's intent for diversity).

Examine How Racial Distance Is Etched into Our Social Landscape

Begin with your local history.

- Search the archives of your public library for articles or documents that provide clues about your neighborhood's history.
- Ask your local realtor for information about the neighborhood where you reside.
- If there is a historical society where you live, inquire about what was going on in your neighborhood prior to your home being built.
- What brought people to that region? What type of housing was made available and to whom? What decisions about roadways and freeways, access points, and transportation were made? How did these decisions impact different groups of people?
- Scan public records online and review city, county, or state deed and census records.
- Look at old maps and photos for a good visual representation of how your community has changed over time.
- Access the *Mapping Inequality* project, which provides digitized historical redlining maps created by the Home Owners' Loan Corporation (HOLC) in the 1930s.

Appendix

- If it is available in your area, take a redlining tour that allows you to understand patterns of exclusion, gentrification, and displacement.
- Have conversations with long-standing residents who have witnessed changes in the neighborhood. Compare the past and present context.
- Who has been part of the local community and in what capacity? Who has been absent? Are there silences in historical documents that suggest intentional or unintentional omission?

Change History's Pattern

Once you've had a chance to understand the historical context of where you live, explore other domains of your life, including your profession, church denomination, and the civic organizations to which you belong. What are the origin stories of these entities? How has race functioned in these realms? Who were the pioneering figures, and what did they believe about racial equality and integration? To what extent are past events and historical legacies part of the present landscape?

If you learn something new about your local context, do something with the information:

- Share it with others. Educate and engage.
- Commit to charting a new path forward. If your profession has a legacy of exclusion and its current makeup reflects that history, lay the groundwork for change. Start local and small by partnering with your school district to create opportunities for early career exposure, mentoring, and job shadowing. Begin in schools with demographics that are underrepresented in your profession.
- Combat stereotypes with information. Dispel assumptions about why certain groups are underrepresented in the various

domains you explored. Where pervasive narratives of "poor individual choices" and "lack of ability" continue to shape expectations, seek a comprehensive account and be willing to dispel myths.

Chapter 6: Know Your Opponent

Surrender Your Social Media to God

Consider how you are using social media outlets. What information are you sharing and receiving? What is it doing to the image of God in others? Is the information edifying or destructive to God's plan for restoration? There is a difference between thoughtful critique and vilification. Thoughtful critique is good. It can raise necessary concerns, offer constructive feedback, and hone our collective understanding. It can also help us to identify brokenness in the world and point us toward faithful action that leads to healing. Vilification, however, pursues the undoing of another person and quickly moves down the path of dehumanizing and violating their inherent dignity, the repercussions of which can be eternal, damaging not only the individual target but our witness to the world. James 3:6 ESV instructs that "the tongue is a fire, a world of unrighteousness . . . set among our members, staining the whole body, setting on fire the entire course of life, and set on fire by hell." Our words emanate from what's in our hearts, and they can bring destruction. Therefore, we must guard our words with diligence and care and with a commitment to glorifying God in all things.

Commit to an Upside-Down Ethic of Love

The kingdom of God is counterintuitive to life in our earthly dwelling place. If we are going to love our enemies, we must learn to live upside down (or what might be right-side up). The heart of this principle is resisting conformity to worldly patterns and choosing forgiveness, mercy, and love over revenge and hatred. When

Appendix

you find yourself ideologically embattled with someone, put down your defenses. Instead, pray. Pray for God to reveal what has been stirred up in your spirit. Is your anger justified? What is the source of your anger? Is it a Godly anger fueled by love? Or is it a prideful anger emanating from a sense of being personally offended?

As you identify the source of your anger, ask God to direct that anger appropriately and use it as a positive catalyst for change. If it is a righteous anger, pray for the ability to act constructively against the wrong, not the wrongdoer. Vengeance is not yours. If it is prideful anger, ask God to heal your heart and start breaking the lies that are fueling your anger.

Pray, too, for compassion toward yourself and the other person, that you might discover your common need for Christ and continue to return to him as your greatest pursuit. When you discover that your only victory in life comes through your daily encounter with God, you will gladly put down your sword. As we trust in God's sovereignty and keep an eternal perspective, we find fewer enemies in our midst. The person we once saw as our opponent becomes a gift as we find opportunity to practice grace and love in action.

Study, Practice, Journal

Read Luke 6:27–36.

- What is the context of this Scripture? What does it mean for us today?

- What does this Scripture tell you about God's expectation for loving your enemies? What is God commanding? How literally do you take these commandments?

- Can you think of a time that you truly loved someone with whom you had a deep divide? What small steps of obedience did you take to get there? What was the evidence of your love? Be specific.

- How did the experience of loving your enemy change you? Your understanding of God?

If you do nothing else after engaging with *Homeward*, take time to study and pray through Matt 5–7. Jesus's Sermon on the Mount is a practical instructional guide that provides daily tools more beneficial than any suggestions I might offer. Take it literally. Use it as a road map for your conversations and interactions and keep a journal of the small changes you notice along the way.

Chapter 7: Remember and Forget, Constructively

Right the Story

Contemplate the stories that shape your understanding of the people groups from whom you are most estranged.

- What incomplete stories have you learned that you need to forget or correct? Can you remember the earliest messages you received about those you struggle with the most?

- What were you taught in school? What did the history books reveal? You may not remember specific details, but what are some of the images or takeaways that come to mind from those early teachings? Were the portrayals mostly positive or negative?

- Can you think of other places where you received messages about those groups, either overtly or implicitly (through television portrayals, the words or actions of family members, or the complete erasure or absence of the groups from authoritative texts)? Have you considered the accuracy or falsehood of those original messages?

- Is there evidence from your lived experience that might suggest the stories were incomplete or misleading? When you discover those deficits, work to rectify them.

Don't allow misinformation to shape your relationships and interactions. Evaluate every received account of various people

Appendix

groups by asking, "How does this align with Gen 1:26–27?" If you cannot reconcile the messages you are receiving with your knowledge that all individuals bear equal dignity and worth in God's created order, then be willing to challenge the information you are receiving. Abandon anything that diminishes the image-bearing humanity of others.

Vision Set and Visualize

Bridging our cultural divides is a particularly formidable endeavor, what leadership expert Ronald Heifetz might refer to as an adaptive challenge.[2] Adaptive challenges are complex and dynamic, resisting solutions that may have worked in the past. And since there is no foreseeable end to tackling societal fragmentation, there must be openness to change and adaptation as the challenges evolve. This kind of work requires something greater than a set of general, unspecified goals and is best galvanized by a life-breathing mission.

As disciples of Christ, our mission is to share the gospel message of salvation, to serve others in love, and reflect God's kingdom on earth. As we commit to a life of worship, surrender, and dependence on the Holy Spirit, we have many good reasons and just as many motivations to pursue healing across racial and cultural differences. So, take some time to name your *why*, to clarify your vision, and visualize the future God is shaping for his people.

Consider what motivated you to read *Homeward* in the first place.

- What is your interest in pursuing healing across the divide?
- Is your pursuit tied to a set of core values, faith convictions, your own personal health and well-being, or a broader commitment to the betterment of society? Perhaps it is all of the aforementioned and some otherwise unmentioned reasons.

We are typically more committed to a goal if we know our *why*, our motivation and reason for pursuing an outcome, so take time

2. Heifetz, *Leadership Without Easy Answers.*

to articulate your mission and create a vision for the kingdom-oriented future you are working toward.

- Are there particular Bible verses that point you to that future?
- If you are committed to a peaceable world, what conditions in your own life need to be present? What relationships do you need to cultivate? How do you need to steward your time and resources? What habits and rituals must you develop to nurture your spirit? Are there things you need to purge or do away with?

As you answer these questions, capture your responses in a vision board and place it somewhere noticeable so you can be reminded each day. Once you set your vision, you can more readily align your behaviors and actions to your desired outcomes and persist through any challenges.

Hold onto God's Promises and Live Accordingly

We know a time is coming when Christ will rule over the entire earth as "King of kings and Lord of lords" (Rev 19:16 ESV). There will be no enmity or strife between people or groups, and all creation will be restored as God intended through the atonement of Jesus Christ. Isaiah 11:6–9 is a reminder that one day we will live peacefully. All we use to protect our individual safety, rights, and prosperity—guns, political agency, legal authority, financial freedom, and territorial claims—will be rendered useless. Instead, we will find ourselves in a new creation where justice and righteousness will reign, where earthly power will crumble under the weight of God's glory, and we will all submit to heaven's perfect will.

In the new creation, God's plan for our greatest good will be carried out, and all disputes will finally be settled. Revelation 21 depicts this new heaven and new earth, the state in which everything is restored, and we dwell together with Christ in perfect unity and wholeness. We are siblings in Christ and will spend eternity together.

Appendix

The question is, "Are we living toward eternity each day, or are we living as if our eternal home is here on earth?" We are to be heaven dwellers now, not tomorrow, not in a future state. Our daily choices and posture can lead us home. May we dwell together in the Lord's redeeming love.

Acknowledgments

I AM GRATEFUL FOR the many individuals who made this book possible.

To my husband, Jon, thank you for your love and support. Thank you for this life together.

To my family, this story doesn't exist without you. Thank you for everything.

To Julia Wattacheril, thank you for the gift of your foreword and friendship. I hold so much admiration for the way you extend God's healing to others.

To Jeff Crosby, your encouragement has meant more than you know. Thank you for championing this work.

To Nathaniel Lee Hansen, the book steward, thank you for being a trusted guide.

To my publisher, thank you for seeing the potential in this book and giving it a home.

To my bernedoodle, Leroy, thank you for being the best early morning writing partner.

To those who remain anonymous but are no less significant in this story, know that your name is etched in my heart.

I am honored and humbled to journey homeward with each of you.

Bibliography

Bartholomew, Craig, and Michael Goheen. *The Drama of Scripture: Finding Our Place in the Biblical Story*. 2nd ed. Grand Rapids: Baker Academic, 2014.

Benjamin, Rich. "The Gated Community Mentality." *New York Times*, March 30, 2012. https://www.nytimes.com/2012/03/30/opinion/the-gated-community-mentality.html.

Bey, Marquis. "'Bring Out Your Dead': Understanding the Historical Persistence of the Criminalization of Black Bodies." *Cultural Studies/Critical Methodologies* 16 (2016). https://journals.sagepub.com/doi/full/10.1177/1532708616634773.

Bonhoeffer, Dietrich. *The Cost of Discipleship*. Translated by R. H. Fuller; edited by Irmgard Booth. New York: Touchstone, 1995.

———. *Life Together: The Classic Exploration of Christian Community*. Translated by John W. Doberstein. New York: HarperOne, 2009.

Brooks, David. *The Second Mountain: The Quest for a Moral Life*. New York: Random House, 2019.

Charles, Mark, and Soong-Chan Rah. *Unsettling Truths: The Ongoing, Dehumanizing Legacy of the Doctrine of Discovery*. Downers Grove, IL: InterVarsity, 2019.

Crouch, Andy. *The Life We're Looking For: Reclaiming Relationship in a Technological World*. New York: Convergent, 2022.

Dowdall, Terry. "Psychological Aspects of the Truth and Reconciliation Commission." In *To Remember and to Heal: Theological and Psychological Reflections on Truth and Reconciliation*, edited by H. Russel Botman and Robin M. Petersen, 27–36. Cape Town: Human & Rousseau, 1996.

Haws, C. G. "Suffering, Hope and Forgiveness: The Ubuntu Theology of Desmond Tutu." *Scottish Journal of Theology* 62 (2009) 477–89.

Heifetz, Ronald A. *Leadership Without Easy Answers*. Cambridge, MA: Belknap, 1994.

Bibliography

Inwood, Joshua, and Derek Alderman. "What If the MLK Holiday Were April 4?" *Diverse Issues in Higher Education*, January 10, 2018. https://www.theeduledger.com/opinion/article/15101847/what-if-the-mlk-holiday-were-april-4.

Jamaica Government Printing Office. *Report of the Commissioners of Inquiry upon the Condition of the Juvenile Population of Jamaica*. Kingston: Government Printing Office, 1879.

Joslin, Wm. P., et al. *Restrictions Covering Plat of Arroyo Vista*. Lot 13, Block 3, July 1, 1946, Deed Book 2501. King County Auditors Deed Volumes, King County Archives, Seattle, WA.

Kaunitz, Todd. "Are You an Arbiter or Distributor of Grace?" Sermon delivered at New Beginnings Church, TX, May 18, 2025.

Keller, Tim. "Jonah and the Mystery of Mercy." Produced by The Gospel Coalition, February 7, 2020. Podcast, 1:02:53. https://www.thegospelcoalition.org/podcasts/tgc-podcast/jonah-and-the-mystery-of-mercy/.

King County Auditors Deed Volumes, King County Archives, Seattle, WA.

King, Martin Luther, Jr. "Letter from Birmingham City Jail." In *A Testament of Hope: The Essential Writings and Speeches of Martin Luther King, Jr.*, edited by James M. Washington, 289–302. New York: HarperOne, 2003.

Lewis, C. S. *A Grief Observed*. New York: HarperOne, 2001.

Mamdani, Mahmood. "Amnesty or Impunity? A Preliminary Critique of the Report of the Truth and Reconciliation Commission of South Africa (TRC)." *Diacritics* 32 (2002) 33–59.

Onwuachi-Willig, Angela. "Policing the Boundaries of Whiteness: The Tragedy of Being 'Out of Place' from Emmett Till to Trayvon Martin." *Iowa Law Review* 102 (2017) 1113–85.

Peck, Raoul, dir. *I Am Not Your Negro*. New York: Magnolia Pictures, 2016.

Rah, Soong-Chan. *Prophetic Lament: A Call for Justice in Troubled Times*. Downers Grove, IL: InterVarsity, 2015.

Reeves, Michael. *Delighting in the Trinity: An Introduction to the Christian Faith*. Downers Grove, IL: IVP Academic, 2012.

Richards Mayo, Sandra. "Chasing the 'Hounds of Hell': Howard Thurman's Jesus and the Disinherited as a Curriculum for Racial Justice and Reconciliation." *Journal of the International Christian Community for Teacher Education* 10 (2015). https://digitalcommons.georgefox.edu/icctej/vol10/iss1/5/.

———. "Know Urban History's Impact." *Response Magazine*, November 2017. https://stories.spu.edu/articles/know-urban-historys-impact.

———. "'Where Riotous Difference Is Welcomed': Reframing Diversity Conversations in Education Through a Theological Understanding of Hospitality." In *The Pedagogy of Shalom: Theory and Contemporary Issues of Faith-Based Education*, edited by HeeKap Lee and Paul Kaak, 45–61. Singapore: Springer, 2017.

BIBLIOGRAPHY

Shaw, Rosalind. *Rethinking Truth and Reconciliation Commissions: Lessons from Sierra Leone*. United States Institute of Peace. Washington, DC: United States Institute of Peace, 2005. https://www.jstor.org/stable/resrep12516.
Smith, David. *Learning from the Stranger*. Grand Rapids: Eerdmans, 2009.
Strain, Justin. "Unity of Command Still Important." Joint Base Charleston, August 16, 2007. https://www.jbcharleston.jb.mil/News/Commentaries/Display/Article/238522/unity-of-command-still-important-principle/.
Thurman, Howard. *Jesus and the Disinherited*. Boston: Beacon, 1996.
———. *Meditations of the Heart*. Boston: Beacon, 1999.
Tripp, Paul. "Your Walk with God Is a Community Project." WTSBooks, April 12, 2011. YouTube. https://www.youtube.com/watch?v=8VpI9zy1yww.
Vanhemert, Kyle. "The Best Map Ever Made of America's Racial Segregation." *Wired*, August 26, 2013. https://www.wired.com/2013/08/how-segregated-is-your-city-this-eye-opening-map-shows-you/.
Wong, May. "Bryan Stevenson Highlights Racism, Inequity in Criminal Justice System in Stanford Talk." *Stanford Report*, January 15, 2016. https://news.stanford.edu/stories/2016/01/openxchange-stevenson-panel-011516.

www.ingramcontent.com/pod-product-compliance
Lightning Source LLC
Chambersburg PA
CBHW022130160426
43197CB00009B/1222